THE PATH OF LEAST RESISTANCE

Principles For Creating What You Want To Create

THE
PATH
OF
LEAST
RESISTANCE

Robert Fritz

STILLPOINT
PUBLISHING

Stillpoint Publishing Company
DMA, Inc.
Technologies for Creating[TM]
27 Congress Street, Salem, MA 01970

Library of Congress Cataloging in Publication Data

Fritz, Robert, 1943–
    The path of least resistance.

    1. Success.   2. Creation (Literary, artistic, etc.)
I. Title
BF637.S8F67   1984   158'.1   84-17512
ISBN 0-913299-34-0

THE PATH OF LEAST RESISTANCE

This book is manufactured in the United States of America. It is designed by Steven A. Baron and the cover photo is by the designer. Composition by Crane Typesetting Service, Barnstable, Massachusetts. Printed and bound by Halliday Lithograph, Inc., Hanover, Massachusetts. Distribution by Stillpoint Publishing, Box 640, Meetinghouse Road, Walpole, NH 03608.

Sixth printing
1987

CONTENTS

ACKNOWLEDGMENTS

Many people have contributed greatly to this book's development. First and foremost is Louis Savary, who helped me bring the book to life. He was not only the major editor but also my major teacher in how to express these ideas in the form of a book.

Kalen Hammann provided extensive, insightful editorial assistance; over three hundred of his suggestions have been incorporated into the present manuscript. Sue King brought materials and people together as she directed the logistics of this project. My wife Rosalind transformed our home into the ideal environment in which to write and was always there to support the effort.

I also acknowledge Peter Senge for the years of discussion and debate about the essence of systems and structure; Charlie Kiefer for his insights and also his help in bringing the book to publication; Robert Hanig for his kind words on the book's jacket; Anita Jaros who as the major typist of the manuscript poured hours into our word processor keeping up with all the changes I continued to make; Kathy Maliawco for typing many of the early chapters; Pat Berne and Jerri Udelson for their suggestions on the manuscript; Robert Shuman for bringing Lou Savary and me together; and Stevan A. Baron for technical production of the book itself.

In addition, my work with the DMA executive staff (Graciela Cummins, Deborah Gold, Kalen Hammann, Robert Hanig, Sheila McGarey, Susan Royal, and David Stanton), as well as with the rest of the DMA staff, DMA local coordinators, and all the DMA instructors throughout the world, is a continuing source of inspiration, profound friendship, and love.

INTRODUCTION

In the early 1960's, as a composition student at The Boston Conservatory of Music, I became aware that there was more to composing music than the techniques of harmony, counterpoint, form, and structure that we were being taught. The art of musical composition seemed to have a meta-musical dimension which at once attracted and mystified me. I wondered what that extra, unseen, unspoken quality was that the great works of art possessed, beyond what could be taught in any conservatory.

Little by little, I began to observe connections between the creative process applied to music, painting, sculpture, dance, drama, film, poetry, and literature and the very same creative process applied to the way people I knew lived their daily lives.

As a composer and musician, I found the creative process endlessly fascinating because in it were integrated a multitude of dimensions of human nature, from the intellectual to the spiritual, the rational to the intuitive, the subjective to the objective, the technical to the metaphysical, the scientific to the religious.

Creators are an enigma to many people, because creators seem to tolerate apparent contradictions quite easily. However, to creators these are not contradictions but opposites which need to be balanced continually, as the bicyclist continually shifts weight from left to right and back again to maintain balance with the least amount of effort. Creators live simultaneously in many universes. Each universe has its own set of governing principles. When a creator performs the creative act, many separate and distinct universes suddenly converge in perfect alignment.

Physicists who work with the time-space continuum tend to open themselves to transcendent and mystical experience as they explore those dimensions more and more deeply. Creators tend to experience a similar kind of opening as separate universes come together to form the single entity which is the fruit of their creation. And so it was natural for me as a composer to search beyond music, to look to all of life for principles of the creative process.

In exploring creativity, I was drawn toward two distinct but related fields: metaphysics and nature. I began to investigate various systems of metaphysics in the early 1960's. I began this investigation with a healthy degree of skepticism. Much of what I found was alloyed with rigid dogma and superstition, both of which I find supremely unattractive to this day. But I also found there some principles which, when applied, release the human spirit in the most powerful of ways. One of the fundamental principles is that there is a direct connection between what occurs in your consciousness and what occurs in your external life, and that if you initiate change internally a corresponding change will happen externally.

When I experimented with this principle, I was astonished by the direct changes that occurred in my life. One immediate change happened with my part-time job.

While a student at The Boston Conservatory, I worked part time at The Town Taxi Company. At 5:30 every morning, I would arrive at the garage, check the oil level of all the company's 120 cabs and add oil as needed. At 8:30 I would rush off to school, only to return to the garage at 4:30 for another three hours, to check the oil level in another fleet of 120 cabs. This was not my all-time favorite job.

About a week after I began to experiment with making inner changes directed toward what I wanted to create, I received a phone call from The New England Conservatory–The Boston Conservatory's main competitor–inviting me to teach in their preparatory department. What was strange was that I knew no one at The New England Conservatory. But they had somehow heard of me and offered me a teaching position. "What a fantastic coincidence!" I thought.

Although I was overjoyed to be in this new job, I gave little serious consideration to the inner experiments I was conducting and the way my new job had come about. But this kind of experience continued to happen. As I instituted inner changes, outer results consistent with what I wanted continued to occur. Although I was skeptical, I was not prejudiced against the idea that these changes had something to do with the inner actions I was taking. In fact, after so many of the inner acts I created became outer results, it would have been irrational for me to deny a relationship between the two, especially since I noticed that when I failed to do the inner work, the outer results did not occur as consistently.

I avoided formulating any theories about how such a connection might actually work. I was not interested in causal theories, but in applied abilities. I was very interested in the process of creating the circumstances of my life that most mattered to me.

Over a period of time, mostly through continued experiments, I began to develop a personal technique of inner creating, which included conceiving of results that I wanted and bringing them into being. Thus, the creative process became part of my normal life.

The second area of vital interest to me involved the laws of physical nature. I spent much time in the woods observing cycles, forces in relation to each other, growth and decay, and how each element of nature affected the other elements to which it was systemically related. I was tremendously excited to find natural principles which I could then use as part of the structure of the music I was composing. Because of these observations, I was able to invent new musical forms and structures, and understand traditional ones, such as the sonata-allegro form, in ways I never had before.

After I received my master's degree in composition, I moved to New York City and then to Los Angeles to work as a musician. During those years, the ability to create the results I wanted was of great importance, for as I did so I am sure I saved myself years which would have been spent building a career in traditional ways.

In 1975, again living in Boston, I was often asked to teach people what I knew about creating. I had no notion then of human development being my life's work, because I was still very active as a professional musician and composer. I phoned a few people I thought would be qualified and suggested to them that they meet each other and put together a course that would teach people to create the lives they wanted. I hoped my friends would develop this course so that I could recommend it to others. When I phoned them again to see what they had produced, they told me they had met and eaten a wonderful Italian dinner, but had not gotten around to discussing the kind of course I had been envisioning. So, I eventually created the course myself.

After I taught the first class, I was hooked. The results the participants were able to create for themselves were, in many cases, miraculous. This was the first DMA course. Shortly after that I founded the DMA organization and developed the Technology for Creating™ curriculum.

Incidentally, the letters D, M and A each have a Kabbalistic meaning. D stands for the Creative Force or Intelligence, M stands for Higher Consciousness, and A stands for the Life Force or Life Breath (prana). Thus the Creative Force, through the vehicle of Higher Consciousness, brings forth the Life Force, or Life Breath.

During this period, I began training others to teach the DMA course, and simultaneously continued to explore what creates real and lasting growth and change in individual lives.

In 1980, I developed a system for observing, understanding, and working with the long-range structural patterns in play in people's lives. This was an important discovery for me, since I had noticed that such patterns seem to produce dysfunctional behavior and results, habitually and predictably. This field of study I named Macrostructural Patterns.

The study of structure has always fascinated me—musical structure, visual structure, systemic structure, and especially the structure of nature and the natural order. When I began to apply structural principles to human development, I found that many of the traditional approaches to growth and human potential only reinforced limiting patterns and often created effects that were quite the opposite of what they were designed to do. This new structural discipline has now been used in psychotherapy with superb results. Many of the patients and clients of psychotherapists using macrostructural patterns report dramatic changes in their lives, changes which previously had seemed impossible.

In the early 1980's, I founded The Institute for Human Evolution, a nonprofit, scientific, and educational organization which has the mandate to further explore, develop, and create structural approaches to human growth in the areas of psychology, psychotherapy, education, and organizational development.

Based on my work with structure and the creative process, in 1981 I made a major revision in the DMA Basic Course. Immediately,

INTRODUCTION

DMA instructors began reporting that their students were creating even more wonderful results and changes in their lives; vastly more important was that these changes were both more fundamental and easier for their students to create. There was something new occurring which had to do with a shift in the basic structures at play–in the ways students were approaching and living their lives. (Currently, there are more than 700 active DMA instructors teaching throughout the United States, Canada, England, Australia, France, Africa, and India, and more than 30,000 graduates of the program.)

I write this book to present to you an entirely different approach to the subject of human development. My frame of reference is not psychological nor what is popularly known as human potential, but rather the creative–the arts. This new approach has made possible to psychotherapists, psychologists, and participants in various human potential workshops something they were never able to reach through their own disciplines–not only a mastery of the creative process (which by itself would be revolutionary), but the ability of the individual to make a shift in fundamental orientation to an entirely separate and unique life stance: the orientation of the creative.

Furthermore, this book is about a new understanding of structure as a dominant factor in the life of the individual, and how the laws of the natural order always move according to structural principles. The major structural principle is known to everyone, and yet is consciously applied by only a few. This principle states that *energy always moves along the path of least resistance*, and that any change you attempt to make in your life will not work if the path of least resistance does not lead in that direction. Throughout this book you will learn to form new structures in your life, which will enable you to direct the path of least resistance where you truly want to go.

PART ONE: FUNDAMENTAL PRINCIPLES

CHAPTER 1

THE PATH OF LEAST RESISTANCE

FORMING THE PATH

People who come to my native Boston often ask me: How did they ever design the layout of the roads in that city? There appears to be no recognizable city planning in Boston, unlike other cities whose streets and avenues are rationally well-organized. The Boston roads were actually formed by utilizing existing cow paths.

But how did these cow paths come to be?

The cow moving through the topography tended to move where it was immediately easiest to move. When a cow saw a hill ahead, she did not say to herself, "Aha! A hill! I must navigate around it." Rather, she put one foot in front of another, taking whichever step was easiest at that moment, perhaps avoiding a rock or taking the smallest incline. In other words, what determined her behavior was the structure of the land.

Each time cows passed through the same area, it became easier and easier for them to take the same path they had taken the last time, because the path began to be more and more clearly defined.

Thus, the structure of the land gave rise to the cows' consistent pattern of behavior in moving from place to place. As a result, city planning in Boston gravitates around the mentality of the 17th century cow.

MOVING ALONG THE PATH

Once a structure exists, energy moves through that structure by the path of least resistance. In other words, *energy moves where it is easiest for it to go.*

[3]

This is true not only for cows, but for all of nature. The water in a river flows following the path of least resistance. The wind blowing through the concrete canyons of Manhattan takes the path of least resistance. Electrical currents, whether in simple devices such as light bulbs or in the complex circuitry found in today's most sophisticated computers, flow along paths of least resistance.

If you watch the flow of pedestrian traffic in time-lapse photography, you can track the patterns of people walking on a busy street avoiding each other on their way. Sometimes a pedestrian's path of least resistance is to walk straight ahead, sometimes to move to the right or left, sometimes to walk faster, sometimes to slow down or wait a moment.

How you got to where you are in your life right now was by moving along the path of least resistance.

THREE INSIGHTS

The rest of this book is built upon three important insights. The first is this:

You are like a river. *You go through life taking the path of least resistance.* We all do—all humans and all of nature. It is important to know that. You may try to change the direction of your own flow in certain areas of your life—your eating habits, the way you work, the way you relate to others, the way you treat yourself, the attitudes you have about life—and you may even succeed for a time. But eventually you find that you return to your original behavior and attitudes—the path of least resistance. This is because your life is determined, insofar as it is a law of nature for you to take the path of least resistance.

The second insight is just as fundamental: *The underlying structure determines the path of least resistance.* Just as the terrain around Boston determined the path of least resistance for the cows to follow, and just as a riverbed determines the path of the water flowing through it, so the structures in your life determine your path of least resistance. Whether you are aware of these structures or not, they are there. The structure of the river remains the same whether there is water flowing through it or not.

You may barely notice the underlying structures in your life, and how powerfully and naturally they determine the way you live.

Many continue to live the way they do, feeling powerless and hopeless. They have attempted to make major changes in their relationships, their careers, their family, their health, and the quality of their lives, only to find themselves, a short time later, back in the same old familiar situation, following their old patterns. They may have indeed made some superficial changes in their lives, but somehow nothing seems really to have changed. They know that there is something more in life, but they don't know how to get to it.

If a riverbed remains unchanged, the water will continue to flow along the path it always has, since that is the most natural route for it to take.

The third insight is this:

We can change fundamental underlying structures of our lives. Just as engineers can change the path of a river by changing the structure of the terrain, so that the river flows where they want it to go, you can change the very basic orientation of your life, so that you can create the life you want.

Furthermore, once a new basic structure is in place, the overall thrust of your life—like the power of the river's current—surges to form the results you truly want. And the direct path to those results becomes the path of least resistance. In fact, with an appropriate change in the underlying structure of your life, the path of least resistance cannot lead anywhere but in the direction you really want to go.

THINKING STRUCTURALLY

To understand the path of least resistance, it is important to understand the concept of structure and what it means to think structurally.

Structure represents the way something is put together. The structure of anything refers to its fundamental parts, how those parts fit together, and how they function in relation to each other and to the whole. A human body's structure refers to its parts–the head, arms, legs, torso, organs, nerves, muscles, etc.–and how they function in relation to each other and to the body as a whole.

To think structurally involves thinking about those fundamental parts and how they function interrelatedly. Physicians and surgeons think structurally about human bodies.

Everything has an underlying unifying structure. Even though you may not consciously think about structure, you presume it. You presume that a building will be structured with walls, floors, ceilings, windows, corridors, stairs, elevators, lighting, plumbing, etc. You would quickly become conscious of a building's structure if it had no stairways or elevators to allow you to get to the upper floors.

The underlying structure directly affects how well a building will function. The underlying structures of your life directly affect how well you function.

OVERCOMING RESISTANCE

I often hear people these days talking about resistance, as if some state of resistance exists in them to which they are a slave. It is as if something they possess overpowers them.

I have heard people say, "I was late because I had resistance to being on time," or "I want to be close and have a good relationship but I have some resistance to it." At a San Francisco dinner party, I even overheard a guest being offered spinach reply, "No, thank you. I have resistance to spinach!"

In those situations, people made an assumption that there was something thwarting them and that what they needed to do was overcome that resistance.

Overcoming resistance makes about as much sense as trying to knock a hole in a wall in order to get into a room. Finding a doorway and stepping through it would be much more efficient.

A psychiatrist once had a patient who experienced resistance in a recurring dream. In the dream, the patient would come to a door and attempt to push it open in order to get through, but the door would not budge. He would keep pushing until he awoke frustrated.

The psychiatrist asked him to imaginatively re-enter the dream scene as it usually happened. As the patient, in his imagination, began once again pushing at the door, the psychiatrist asked him to stop for a moment and look at the door. "See if you can find out anything about the door that will help you get through," he encouraged.

"There's some writing on the door," the man said.

"What does it say?" asked the psychiatrist.

The man replied, "It says . . . . . it says . . . . . 'Pull!' "

The man in his dreams had made the assumption that doors must always be pushed open. He had also concluded that the door was resisting him opening it. Based on his assumption, he believed that his individual path of least resistance was to try to push or break through the door.

The man was inadvertently imposing on reality his notion of how doors work. By doing that, he kept himself from discovering how that particular door worked.

People often attempt to impose on reality their notion of how it universally works. Often it works differently from the way they had assumed. By imposing their own assumptions on reality, they greatly limit their own possibilities in life.

It is not your resistance that keeps you from the results you want, nor is it anything you need to overcome. It is the structures presently at play in your life that determine what your path of least resistance is and will be.

Whether a man moving through the corridors of a building to get to an appointment jumps, skips, hops, runs, or walks there, the structure of the building remains unchanged and, therefore, so does the path of least resistance. If the man tries to move through a solid wall, he meets "resistance."

Overcoming resistance will not work because the basic structure of the building is still in play and, in fact, its influence is reinforced by any attempt on the man's part to overpower it.

When you attempt to overcome resistance in your life, you merely reinforce the underlying structure in play. By focusing on the resistance, like the man trying to get through the solid wall, you empower the resistance, and it becomes more important than the result you want.

People on a diet often focus on their resistance to dieting. They remind themselves how hungry they are, how much they miss ice cream, how much they miss cocktails, how bored they are with the limited selection of food the diet allows, how much trouble the process is, and how they are always thinking about food. In fact, the harder they try to stop thinking about food, the more they think about it. Despite all their efforts to overcome their resistance to the diet, they become totally focused on their resistance.

Many people use willpower to try to overpower their problems. But the more they try to improve their lives in this way, the more entrenched in their problems they become. Some dieters tend to become more and more frustrated, yet more and more determined, as they try to overcome their resistance to the diet.

Other people attempt to make changes in their lives—and do in fact change their circumstances to a degree—only to find themselves ending up in a situation similar to the one from which they started.

Tom left his first marriage partly because he and his wife seemed incompatible. She never seemed interested in anything he cared about. When he married Lynn, his second wife, he thought that this time he was with a mate who shared his interests and ideals. After three years, however, Lynn had developed interests and ideals of her own, which were very different from Tom's. And Tom found himself once again in the familiar situation of having a wife whose interests were incompatible with his own.

The life experiences you now have are a natural outcome of the structures you have previously established in your life. The path of least resistance in those structures has led you to where you now are and what you now have.

DYNAMIC AND OPEN STRUCTURES

Although some structures in the physical world are already fixed and set, such as the structure of the Prudential Building in Boston or the Empire State Building in New York, most of the structures that we deal with in our lives are dynamic, flexible, and open.

Language constantly puts you in touch with your ability to create dynamic and open structures. Every time you write or speak you build a dynamic structure called a sentence, which in English is made up of a subject, verb, often an object, prepositional phrases, modifiers, etc.

Unless you understand the basic structures of your native language, you cannot hope to communicate effectively with anyone, except on the most primitive level. Unless you know how to create and change the basic structures of your life, you cannot hope to create the life you want.

You think structurally whenever you fill a glass with water. The elements of the structure are the glass, the water, the faucet controlling the flow of water, how much water you want in the glass, and how much water is actually in the glass.

All of these separate elements are in a single structural system. Each element is related to other elements in the system, and each element is related to the whole system.

When you fill a glass you have a goal. The goal is the glass filled with the *desired amount* of water. You also have an awareness of the current situation: how much water is presently in the glass. If there is less water in the glass than the amount you desire, there will be a discrepancy in the system. This discrepancy will be lessened by adding water which you do by controlling the faucet. As the current amount of water approaches the desired amount of water, you close the faucet by degree, slowing down the flow of water, and stopping it entirely when the present amount of water is the same as the desired amount of water, thus ending the discrepancy.

Filling a glass of water may take only seconds, but within that time a structural system is in play, involving all of the elements within that system.

CHANGING UNWANTED STRUCTURES

Once you begin to think structurally about your life, you probably will be able to identify an unwanted underlying structure. Once you identify such a structure, you have the opportunity to change it.

As long as unwanted life-structures remain unchanged, you will always tend to gravitate back to old familiar patterns, no matter how much you want to change your life or how hard you try.

In this book I will focus on helping you establish new and effective underlying life-structures. Then the most natural tendency–the path of least resistance–will lead you to a fulfilling and satisfying life.

As you establish these new structures in your life, not only does

[9]

what you most deeply want become possible, it becomes probable.

No one can know who might suddenly emerge as a force to change the course of a society. At age 26, in 1955, Martin Luther King, Jr., was a quiet, introverted intellectual minister whose major pursuit was scholarly research.

But one day in that same year in a church in Montgomery, Alabama, in the very beginning of the civil rights bus boycott, King rose to champion justice and freedom. In that single gesture his life-orientation changed from scholar to leader. From that moment on he became one of the major catalysts in changing the history of America.

Standing at the pulpit, looking out over a row of television cameras and a fully packed church, King eloquently and poetically described the reality of the moment.

> There comes a time when people get tired. We are here this evening to say to those who have mistreated us all along that we are tired—tired of being segregated and humiliated, tired of being kicked about by the brutal feet of oppression. For many years we have shown amazing patience. We have sometimes given our white brothers the feeling that we liked the way we were being treated. But we come here tonight to be saved: to be saved from the patience that makes us patient with anything less than freedom and justice.

King spoke for sixteen minutes extemporaneously. Until that moment, no one had ever made a speech like this, which so poignantly and powerfully expressed the discrepancy between the current situation and a clear vision of freedom and justice. King ended his speech by saying:

> If we protest courageously and yet with dignity and Christian love, when the history books are written in the future, somebody will have to say, "There lived a race of people, of black people, of people who had the moral courage to stand up for their rights, and thereby they injected a new meaning into the veins of history and civilization."

At this point in the history of our civilization, social and cultural structures are in transition. The structures emerging as a result of this shift in the times will enable you to increase your ability to create new life-structures for yourself, and support you in living up to your highest potential and purpose, as they did for Martin Luther King, Jr.

A SHIFT IN THE TIMES

A SHIFT OF DOMINANCE

With the coming of any new period in history, new principles become dominant. With the birth of the United States during The Age of Reason, the new principle that became dominant was freedom of the individual. This principle became a fundamental part of the structure of our civilization.

In all of recorded history the concept of individual freedom had never been dominant. By becoming dominant in the Revolutionary Period it enabled people to rearrange entirely the basic premises by which they lived their lives and organized their societies.

When a new principle shifts into dominance in any historical period, the underlying structure of the civilization changes. Once the underlying structures change, the major thrust of human energy and power moves along a new path of least resistance, and great changes in civilization burst forth.

In the 18th century, the founders of the United States inserted in the new constitution a Bill of Rights, which not only granted but guaranteed individuals freedom to assemble, freedom to worship, freedom of the press, and freedom from self-incrimination.

In the 16th century, freedom of the individual was not impossible, it was simply not the path of least resistance of the times. In the tide of history beginning in the 18th century, however, the path of least resistance led toward viewing the individual as a significant entity.

A few hundred years ago slavery was taken for granted in the United States. At that time, a politician who favored slavery was considered to have a legitimate viewpoint. Today, if a politician advocated slavery, he would be laughed and jeered out of politics.

A NEW DOMINANT PRINCIPLE

In our period of time, there is a shift of dominance to a new principle. The new principle is that *you as an individual are the predominant creative force in your life.*

This means that the predominant activity in your life will no longer be reacting or responding to events as they occur. Rather, it will be creating the life you want.

The emphasis will no longer be placed on mastery of more and more sophisticated ways of responding–how to be assertive, how to solve your problems, how to deal with conflicts, how to confront others, how to manipulate others, how to protect yourself, how to say what you really feel. Rather, the emphasis will be on *mastery of the creative process–how to bring into reality the results you truly want to create.*

People have always symbolized the human being in different ways. Aristotle was probably first to symbolize the self as a "rational animal." Others have symbolized the self in terms of emotions, socio-economic status, race, skin color, religion, or nationality.

Today for the most part we symbolize ourselves as *responders* to people and events. Responders characteristically use familiar expressions such as "How do you feel about him?" or "How are you going to respond to what she did?" or "What's your reaction to that?"

The new emerging dominant principle will re-symbolize the self as a creator, so that in human activity creativity will hold primacy.

"Creation is the paramount symbol that is being disclosed in our time," writes theologian Gibson Winter in *Liberating Creation* (Crossroad, 1981). "The self can best be resymbolized in the context of the creative process."

The shift of dominance from a life of *responding to what occurs* to a life of *creating what will be* invites us to focus on vision and new possibilities.

This shift of dominance will bring with it not only new possibilities but also new requirements, new abilities to master, new experiences in which to become fluent, and a new life-orientation. As this new principle becomes dominant, it will enable people to rearrange the basic premises by which they live their lives and organize society.

What will support and inspire us to meet the new challenge is the underlying shift in the structure of the times. Also, the new path of least resistance will most naturally lead toward mastering new requirements, developing new fluency, and shaping a new life-orientation.

At this moment in history, we are poised to make this shift; that is, we are in the position of utmost readiness. All the external elements–high technology, mass communication, etc.–that need to be in play for this shift to happen are ready. That these elements do exist in readiness redefines the nature of our age.

MAKING THE SHIFT

In the long history of our planet, we have witnessed many attempts to institute changes which were designed to bring about a more rewarding and fulfilling life. We have seen changes in political and economic systems, changes in geographical borders and world leaders, changes in technology and theories.

While some of these systems are better than others, the general approach of changing external circumstances in an attempt to change the human condition has enormous built-in limitations.

Unfortunately, the popular message that society delivers is that a change in external circumstances is all that is needed to enable us to have a rewarding and fulfilling life. We often hear,

"If only we had a guaranteed annual wage."
"If only there were no Communists."
"If only we had different people in power."
"If only we changed the tax structure for large corporations."
"If only we had socialized medicine."
"If only we had arms control."
"If only I were more beautiful."
"If only people treated me better."
"If only I had more money."

Behind each of these wishes in the "responder's" mind is the belief that the changed circumstances would somehow automatically

[14]

produce a fulfilling life, and that all people would have to do to enjoy that life is respond appropriately to the changed external circumstances.

However, *when you make the shift to being the predominant creative force in your life, you move from reacting and responding to the external circumstances of your life to creating directly the life you truly want.*

In every age in history there has been a small proportion of individuals who seem to have made this shift, mastered their inner creative process and, because of that, advanced civilization by their creations.

Albert Einstein, Pablo Picasso, Jane Addams, Alexander Graham Bell, Marie Curie, Thomas Edison, Charles Darwin, Sigmund Freud, Margaret Sanger, Ludwig Von Beethoven, Michaelangelo, Eleanor of Aquitaine, J. S. Bach, Raphael, Francis Bacon, Benjamin Franklin, Thomas Jefferson, Margaret Mead, Martin Luther King, Jr., Mary Wollstonecraft, and Mohandas Gandhi are some of the individuals who have mastered their inner creative process and in their own way made a lasting mark on our civilization.

HUMANITY AS A WHOLE

What is new about our age is that the very times in which we live are conducive to humanity as a whole making this shift and mastering the inner creative process.

In his book *Megatrends*, John Naisbitt points out that one of today's megatrends is that the individual is looking less to be taken care of by large institutions and more toward self-reliance.

Civilization's shift to the individual as the predominant creative force is even more than a megatrend. It is part of the historic evolutionary pattern, similar to the shift in prehistoric times from a hunting society to an agricultural one, to the shift from collective identity to the concept of privacy, and to the shift from the divine right of kings to the freedom of the individual.

The historic period in which we live is a period of reawakening to a commitment to higher values, a reawakening of individual purpose, and a reawakening of the longing to fulfill that purpose in life.

A predominant phenomenon of the past few decades has been widespread disillusionment and disappointment with life, which in many ways had its origins in the idealism of the 1960's. Because of that disillusionment, many people buried their dreams, denied what they longed for and deeply cared about, and suppressed what most mattered to them.

With the current reawakening of vision and purpose, life begins to take on new possibilities. No period in human civilization has provided such possibilities for planetary change. Moreover, in no period of human history before now has each individual had such a possibility of directly influencing the course and destiny of our civilization.

With the new dominant principle of the individual as the predominant creative force, you may find yourself able to assume a new authority in helping set the direction for the new civilization which is emerging. This authority does not stem from a naive utopianism, but is steeped in the structural tendencies of the time.

Within the fundamental shift in the underlying structure of civilization now taking place, the path of least resistance is leading individuals toward aspiring to what is truly highest in the vision of humanity.

Although the path before us is filled with challenges, these are truly the most exciting times ever to be alive.

THE STARTING POINT

To make any shift, you need to know your starting point. For most people, the starting point is an orientation toward life that I call *reactive-responsive*.

The following chapter outlines the essential structure of this orientation which is now commonly in play in people's lives. In this orientation, the path of least resistance often leads to unwanted outcomes.

Subsequent chapters will help enable you to make the shift to the new orientation in which you become the dominant creative force in your life.

This shift, however, can only be made by you, for yourself. No matter how much I or anyone else would wish the shift for you, it is truly personal and uniquely yours.

CHAPTER 3

THE REACTIVE-RESPONSIVE ORIENTATION

LOOKING TO THE EXTERNAL

Before this time in history, the concept of human advancement was focused on sources outside the individual. Statesmen shaped the governments that ruled us. Scientists evolved the theories that shaped our industrialized society. Technicians in the giant corporations designed the tools, appliances, electronics, and vehicles that shaped our daily lives. Learned professors wrote the books that were designed to shape our minds. Psychologists applied the therapeutic processes that were designed to shape our emotional lives. Medical science formulated approaches that were designed to restore our health. The forces that shaped our lives then were seen as external to ourselves. A common assumption was that, if outer circumstances were changed, the inner experience of individuals and groups would also change.

Some people believed that if we changed outer circumstances so that we had adequate housing, adequate health care, a shorter work week, inexpensive rapid transportation, smaller families, and so on, individuals would be happier, healthier, more well-balanced, and psychologically secure.

The fact is that many people do have adequate housing, adequate health care, and the rest, yet they are still unhappy, unhealthy, unstable, and psychologically insecure.

In the early 20th century, the American composer Charles Ives took much of his philosophical and aesthetic inspiration from Henry Thoreau. But Ives did point out one major disagreement he had with this philosopher. Thoreau believed that if people returned to living in the natural environment of the woods, they would automatically develop an innate transcendental spiritual orientation. Ives observed that most of the people he knew who had lived for generations under natural circumstances in the wooded hills of West Virginia and Tennessee had yet to reach this transcendental state. Instead, Ives noted, they mostly thought of themselves as hillbillies.

Here, Thoreau had assumed that changing the outward circumstances would change people's inner experiences. Charles Ives observed that it did not.

While people's reactions and responses changed radically as a result of new external circumstances such as political revolutions and technological breakthroughs, their underlying assumptions remained essentially unchanged. They continued to assume that the predominant creative force in their lives was external to them; it came from somewhere other than themselves.

For example, while the Industrial Revolution produced great shifts of population and a reorganization of the social structure of 19th Century Europe, the predominant factor that determined the life and destiny of the individual was still external circumstances, just as it had been during the feudal periods and just as it has remained until our day.

Today, whether you are a farmer, a factory worker, a manager, an industrialist or a stock broker, the power in your life is too often perceived to lie in all of the external circumstances to which you need to respond, or against which you need to react.

LOOKING TO THE INTERNAL-EXTERNAL

In the reactive-responsive orientation, there are certain internal circumstances such as fear, anger, illness, or parts of the personality that are treated the same as if they were external circumstances. They are seen as internally external: "I had so much anger, I had to leave the room" or "My fear got in the way in my job interview" or "My relationship with my father was incomplete, so I can't seem to have a good relationship with a man" or "My mind gets in the way when I am trying to be spontaneous" or "My ego gets me in trouble" or

"I need to overcome my sinful nature" or "My stomach rebels against spicy food."

These are all examples of internal circumstances which, to some people, function as if they were external circumstances. That is, people react or respond to these internal circumstances as if they were beyond their reach or control. While these circumstances are in fact primarily inner and self-referential, they function for the reactive-responsive person as if they were originating somewhere beyond the personal sphere of influence. In the reactive-responsive orientation, these internal circumstances seem to demand attention in exactly the same way outward circumstances might.

Thus, certain internal circumstances as well as external circumstances are seen by people in the reactive-responsive orientation as being beyond their direct control.

In talking about the reactive-responsive orientation, I call "circumstantial stimuli" any stimuli, external or internal, which seem to force people to take action.

CIRCUMSTANTIAL STIMULI

One way to describe the reactive-responsive orientation is as a way of living in which you predominantly react or respond to circumstantial stimuli beyond your direct control. When things change in your circumstances, you react or respond to what just changed.

Some circumstantial stimuli appear friendly and welcome; others seem adversarial and unwelcome. "She smiled at me, and suddenly I felt more comfortable." "He looked away, and I began to feel insecure." "When my son dropped the dish and broke it, I couldn't stop yelling at him for five minutes." "The salesman seemed sincere, so I bought the dishwasher." "Because I ate the candy bar, I typed faster for the next twenty minutes."

While at times circumstantial stimuli evoke spontaneous reactions, at other times they seem to call for "appropriate" responses. "She had the flu, so I thought it was a good idea to bring her chicken soup." "The workmen did not do a good job, so I felt justified in bringing suit against them." "They invited me to the party so warmly that I had to say yes." "He was so bad, I had to get divorced. What would you have done?"

In each of these cases it seemed to the persons involved that the circumstantial stimuli caused their reaction or response. The power to influence their actions in each situation was attributed to the circumstances, which in some way or other forced or impelled them to take action.

In these examples the persons took action based on the assumption that it was circumstances out of their direct control which somehow demanded that they do something. Their only choice in the matter was limited to how to respond or react to what had just happened. They did not feel they could choose what they wanted, independent of circumstances.

In the reactive-responsive orientation, it always seems that circumstances are powerful—more powerful than you are. You feel that all you can do is to react or respond to them. Even if you have developed great skill in outmaneuvering circumstances, like a lion tamer outmaneuvering his lions, it is still the circumstances—the lions—which hold the ultimate control in how you live your life.

A STRATEGY OF AVOIDANCE

When Joni arrived at the party at 10:30 p.m., the room was already filled with music and guests. The host greeted her and led her over to the table where the food and wine were spread out.

As Joni filled her plate with hors d'oeuvres and her glass with Bordeaux, she was scanning the room to see whom she wanted to avoid. This was the first thing she always did in large groups.

When Grace began to walk toward her, Joni pretended not to see her and walked through the crowd in the opposite direction, smiling and saying hello to various people.

Just when she began to feel a sense of relief about avoiding Grace, she found herself walking directly toward an old friend, Eddie, who was sitting in the corner. She knew that Eddie, who was always filled with self-pity, would monopolize her time if he could, complaining about his life. So before she reached Eddie she called a quick hello to him, and took a sharp left turn.

Another old acquaintance, Jack, always good humored, was just finishing telling a joke to two other people. Joni slipped in between them, in time to hear the punch line and join in the laughter.

During the rest of the party, Joni seemed to be living on nerves and feelings. She avoided engaging in most conversations because she felt she did not know how to relate to the stylish people there, who were talking about exotic vacation spots and esoteric metaphysics. Instead, she stayed on the edge of things and mostly remained silent.

Eventually, she found herself in conversation with an attractive man who seemed to show an interest in her. When he seemed ready to extend an invitation, so that they could see each other again, she quickly changed the subject to "automobiles." It was her way to avoid having to decide whether or not to get involved with him.

At the party, Joni was again and again using a reactive-responsive strategy designed to move around or away from unwelcome circumstances as they occurred. In the reactive-responsive orientation, avoidance strategies of this kind are common.

In these strategies the focus is on what you want to avoid, and the usual action is trying to make sure it doesn't happen. If you worry chronically, your worry is an avoidance strategy designed to prevent or avoid the negative consequences about which you are worrying. Some people worry about getting ill, others worry about being disapproved of, others about being fired from their jobs, others about being rejected by friends, others about being made the center of attention, and so on. In each case, the focus is on what they do not want, and their strategy is designed to force them into taking preventative action.

Look at your life and notice what you are avoiding and what actions you are taking to prevent negative consequences.

There are people who stay in a relationship only to avoid the uncertainty of a new lifestyle without their partner.

There are people who leave a relationship only to avoid dealing with the anger, resentment, and discouragement which might come from staying within it.

For some, the decision to stay in a relationship or to leave it depends on what is the biggest discomfort to avoid—the uncertainty of a new life or the resentment building up in the present one. No matter what they decide, they make their choice based on the assumption that all they can do is react or respond to the circumstances.

THE PRE-EMPTIVE STRIKE

In the reactive-responsive orientation, even more common than the strategy designed to avoid immediate unwanted circumstances is a longer-range strategy designed to prevent unwanted circumstances from happening in the first place. This latter strategy is called a *pre-emptive strike*.

At the party, Joni was using a strategy to avoid immediate unwanted circumstances. In fact, it was practically all she did during the party.

After a number of similar unwelcome experiences like that party, Joni may decide not to attend any more parties. Such a strategy on her part, designed to *prevent* the discomfort she might experience at a party from happening, would be a pre-emptive strike. If Joni never accepted an invitation to any more parties, she would never find herself in those circumstances again.

The pre-emptive strike takes many forms. Some people develop assertive personalities, as a pre-emptive strike to avoid being manipulated by others. At meetings, some people publicly criticize themselves, as a pre-emptive strike to prevent being criticized by anyone else. Some act insecure and irresponsible, in a pre-emptive strike to prevent having demands placed upon them. Some people act arrogantly and unfriendly, in a pre-emptive strike to prevent closeness and intimacy. Some get upset and hurt easily, in a pre-emptive strike to prevent being confronted by anyone. Some put themselves in situations in which they appear to be victimized, as a pre-emptive strike to prevent being taken advantage of. Some people dedicate their time and energy to selfless deeds, as a pre-emptive strike to avoid ever having to deal with suspicions they may have about their own selfishness.

A subtle pre-emptive strike may turn out to be a lifelong strategy. You may have learned, early on, the kinds of situations that could be threatening to you, and gradually developed strategies to prevent them from ever occurring in your life again.

Certain people may point to their life circumstances and say, "I live a charmed life," or "My life is full of contentment," or "My life is happily normal and well-balanced." Even though these people may describe their lives as "good," a more accurate description for the lives of some of them would be "unburdened by conflict." The way their lives became conflict-free was through elaborate avoidance strategies learned along the way, whenever they found themselves in unwanted situations.

Today, Frank earns a six-figure annual salary and considers himself financially secure. But he grew up in a very poor family, where his parents worried and fought with each other about the precarious state of their family finances. When Frank went to school, he always felt embarrassed about his hand-me-down clothes. Out of embarrassment, he never invited his friends to his house. And he often could not afford the extra-curricular activities offered at school. Any money he earned in his spare time he had to contribute to the family.

Frank always thought of himself as poor. Even when he was first married, although he was already earning a good living, he budgeted the family finances very carefully, even down to the smallest details such as items on the grocery bill. Over the years, he struggled to save as much money as he could to build financial security.

Even after Frank became financially strong, earning more than one-hundred-thousand dollars a year, he carefully budgeted every dollar. He steered clear of any magazine article, television program, or newspaper column on the subject of poverty. Whenever one of his high school friends invited him to a wedding or a dinner party, he never went. His circle of friends came to include only people who grew up in well-to-do families. One exception to Frank's frugality at home was the way he showered his children with presents and money. He made sure they wore the best quality clothes, even when they did not want to. He encouraged his children to invite their friends over to the house, and had a game room built especially for them.

Frank usually described his life as comfortable and good.

Actually, with Frank there was always an undercurrent of insecurity. For the life circumstances he had created around himself were an elaborate pre-emptive strategy to avoid poverty. Frank had an ulterior motive in creating his secure financial situation: to never be poor again.

Within Frank's orientation toward life, no amount of money in the world would be enough to buy him financial independence, because he carried his poverty with him in his consciousness all through life.

[23]

ON THE DEFENSIVE

Most of Frank's career decisions were made as a pre-emptive strike to prevent poverty. The way he treated his children was a pre-emptive strike to prevent their having the kinds of experiences he had as a child. His obsession with the household budget was a pre-emptive strike to prevent any waste of money. His avoidance of reading about poverty or viewing television programs about poverty was a pre-emptive strike designed to keep him from reminding himself of his past circumstances, as was his refusal to see his high school friends.

Some people who enjoy better than ordinary lives base their lives on an avoidance strategy which permeates many of their actions and attitudes. They manage to reach a certain plateau of insulation, keeping themselves "safe" and "certain."

You might be thinking, "What's wrong with that? After all, people like Frank live comfortably and are safe. What's wrong with living like that?"

There is nothing inherently wrong with Frank having an affluent life, but any aspirations he may have are motivated by an avoidance of poverty. In a sense, his life spirit is chained by his pre-emptive strategies, and all his energy is focused on what he doesn't want.

Such people are continually in a position of potentially compromising whatever they may truly want in their lives for the sake of safety, security, and a sense of peace. Through this defensive strategy, the most they can hope to attain in their lives is complacency and mediocrity. Underneath all their security, there is an undercurrent of dissatisfaction and vulnerability to circumstances beyond their direct control.

Many of these people eventually become cynical about life. Others become stoical. Still others, like Frank, become committed to a pretense of happiness, while underneath it all they experience lack of fulfillment. All of them suffer from the price they pay in not being true to themselves.

Years of living avoidance strategies gradually undermines their sense of power. No matter what situations they have created to shield themselves from unwanted circumstances, they are left powerless. While Frank might appear to his friends to be in a position of power, mostly what he experiences is unending powerlessness, due to his constant need to control his life circumstances in an effort to prevent the poverty he fears. While on the surface Frank appears to be self-assured, deep inside he is actually engaged in a lifelong struggle–always on the defensive–against poverty and feeling powerless and thus driven to succeed.

THE PREMISE OF POWERLESSNESS

The reactive-responsive orientation contains the basic premise that you are powerless. If you predominantly react or respond to circumstantial stimuli, where does the power lie in these situations? It clearly lies outside you, in the circumstances or the stimuli. Therefore, since the power does not reside in you, you are powerless.

Even among those who have achieved what most people would consider great success, many have obtained that success in order to avoid failure. Success itself does nothing to change the premise of powerlessness.

Others keep themselves from success to avoid the unwanted consequences they think success will bring them. For example, there are people who stay in jobs they don't like–sometimes in circumstances that are quite painful–to avoid the insecurity and problems a new job might bring.

When people are in a reactive-responsive orientation, whatever the outcome–whether success or failure–they will always feel incomplete and unsatisfied. The only difference between those who have achieved the success they sought and those who have not is that the "successful" ones know that their success has not brought them the deep experience of satisfaction and fulfillment they really want. Their success is an empty victory.

REACTIVE-RESPONSIVE EDUCATION

Most people in our society were nurtured and trained within a reactive-responsive orientation.

Much of what you learned growing up was what not to do and what to avoid. The majority of the behavioral rules you were given as a child were based on avoidance or prevention. "Don't play in the street." "Don't bother your father." "Don't play with matches." "Don't be late."

In one psychological study, three- and four-year-old children had small tape recorders attached to them which recorded everything they were told. After analyzing the tapes, researchers discovered that 85 percent of what children were told was about either what they couldn't do or how bad they were because of what they were doing.

Since parents want children to avoid negative consequences, it is not surprising that the elaborate avoidance strategies they teach live long after children know how to cross the street or light a match safely.

Unfortunately, most educational systems also reinforce a reactive-responsive orientation. One focus of education is to weave the child into the fabric of society. This means the school takes on the job of teaching the student how to respond. Most students adapt well and learn how to respond "appropriately."

Some young people, however, reject the imposition of what seem to them to be arbitrary values and behavior, and react against the circumstantial stimuli of their education. For the most part schools, like parents, teach children either to react or respond.

THE WAY LIFE IS

One of the basic premises in the reactive-responsive orientation is that "life is a certain way and your job is to negotiate around the way life is."

Parents and teachers tell children what to do and what not to do in order to help children be accepted and secure in the family and in society. Children may cooperate or rebel, but it is clear to them that the adult's job is to know how life is. This implies to children that things are a certain way, that the certain way is knowable, that this is important knowledge, that one is better off knowing than not knowing how things are, and that one ought to find out how things are so one can respond appropriately.

The power in the situation is clearly defined as being in the school (or the parents). So the students are really learning about power. What they learn about power is that they are powerless.

They are also learning about their purpose in life. Unfortunately, what they learn is that they are only an insignificant one among many, and that they need to conform. Under those conditions, what purpose or meaning does their life ultimately have?

RESPONSIVE BEHAVIOR: GOOD STUDENTS AND NICE PEOPLE

If you go along with the notion that things are the way you were told they are, and act appropriately—I call this responsive behavior—you might be labeled a "good student" or a "nice person."

Responsive students usually receive good grades in school and actively adapt to the norms and standards set by people in positions of authority. As adults, they continue to be taught to respond in a variety of ways. In many approaches to the "development of human potential," for instance, people are actually encouraged to learn new and more sophisticated ways of responding to how life is.

This is a trap, however, because that which at first seems to free them ultimately binds them. Such approaches as releasing repressed areas of consciousness, positive thinking, transformational experiences, accepting things exactly the way they are, "creative" problem solving, situational management, behavior modification, stress reduction, and even certain forms of meditation, all attempt to teach people how to respond to life or the universe as it is. After years of practicing these various disciplines, people often have not mastered how to create what they most truly want. What they have learned is only how to respond and adapt.

REACTIVE BEHAVIOR: REBELLIOUS STUDENTS AND DIFFICULT PEOPLE

Other people actively oppose society's message that things are the way they are portrayed at home or in school, and behave rebelliously. I call their behavior reactive. Reactive people are usually labeled "rebellious students" or "difficult people."

If you are reactive, it is not that you don't believe life and things are a certain way. You do. But the way you believe things are is not necessarily the way society is presenting them to you.

A common experience is not having a situation or circumstance to your liking, either at home, at school, at work, or in a social setting, or simply while engaged in an activity like driving. You may express a direct intolerance of some circumstance by being actively rebellious and disruptive. Or you may shift from overt to covert behavior, what is commonly called passive-aggressive behavior, by being late, not keeping agreements, or breaking the law, but attempting to be inconspicuous about it. As one student who recalled being reactive put it, "I followed enough rules to get by, but I deliberately violated any rules I could get away with."

Speaking of rebellious students and difficult people reminds me of a management group in a successful high-tech corporation I once visited. The meeting began when someone in the group made a simple and obviously true statement, something like, "We need to come to some agreement about the budget for this new project."

At that point, an argument broke out and the entire group began fighting. They demanded reasons why the simple statement was true. The man who made the statement was forced to come up with a number of reasons to defend his position.

After forty minutes of arguing, with expressions of fierce antagonism, the group finally decided that, in fact, they needed to come to agreement about the budget for the new project.

They had spent so much energy establishing that simple fact that they were exhausted and couldn't discuss anything else that morning. The psychological tension and anxiety in the group were so high that if someone had introduced another opening statement, there would probably have been another forty minutes of arguing. They were out to get one another. They played their games of entrapment, sometimes being polite, reasonable, and nice; at other times being stubborn, temperamental, and explosive.

It was astonishing to be in the presence of this group of people and to see how reactively they operated. I was later told, "They are among the best-behaved groups within the company."

A reactive orientation in life is common and familiar in everyone's experience. Examples of reactive behavior are found in many marriages, work situations, family relationships, and social interactions.

Most people learn to respond appropriately. Society considers the educational process a success when reactive people graduate to being responsive ones.

THE REACTIVE-RESPONSIVE ORIENTATION: NICE AND DIFFICULT PEOPLE

Nice, responsive people build up resentment over time because of their chronic position of powerlessness. When enough resentment is built up, they turn into difficult, reactive people. But since that change does nothing to enhance their position with regard to power and, in fact, feels disorienting, they return to being nice, responsive people.

On the other hand, difficult, reactive people create so much commotion that, over a period of time, they build up guilt as well as resentment because of their chronic destructiveness and powerlessness. When enough guilt is built up, they repent and turn into nice, responsive people. Next, they build up the resentment nice, responsive people feel, usually in a short time, and then return to being difficult, reactive people.

Some people spend most of their time in the responsive mode, with temporary shifts into the reactive. Others spend most of their time in the reactive mode, with temporary shifts into the responsive. The history of many individuals is the story of moving back and forth between reactive and responsive.

Throughout these shifts, although the behaviors, actions, policies, and even philosophies may be changed, the underlying structural pattern of either responding or reacting to circumstantial stimuli is still the game being played.

A CLOSED AND CIRCULAR SYSTEM

If your orientation is primarily in a responsive mode, the path of least resistance is to move to the reactive. But once there, the path of least resistance leads you back to the responsive.

If your orientation is primarily in a reactive mode, the path of least resistance is to move to the responsive. But once there, the path of least resistance leads you back to the reactive.

If it seems to you that this is a closed and circular system, you are right. If you attempt to solve, change, break through, transform, accept, reject or avoid this structure, all you will do is reinforce it. As long as you try to make changes from within the reactive-responsive orientation, you will of course remain within that orientation.

I caution you against attempting prematurely to make a shift into the orientation of the creative, because chances are you will be acting from the reactive-responsive orientation and, as a result, not only will it not work but you will also be reinforcing that orientation.

The President of DMA, Inc., Dr. Kalen Hammann, has said, "If you find yourself in a hole, stop digging." If you prematurely attempt to make the shift to the orientation of the creative, motivated by the discomfort of circumstantial stimuli, you are merely digging yourself into a deeper hole.

If one cannot solve or change this reactive-responsive orientation in any way, what is left to do?

The answer is to do nothing to alter it until you have a deeper understanding of some of the structural mechanisms in play and how they work. In this way, you are preparing yourself for a successful shift into a new orientation, in which you master the principle of the path of least resistance and truly become the predominant creative force in your own life.

CHAPTER 4

STRUCTURAL CONFLICT

STRUCTURAL TENDENCIES

Structural tendencies are directions the path of least resistance tends
to take as it moves through the structure.

For example, the structural tendency of a stretched rubber band
is to move from a state of tension (being stretched) to a state of
resolution (being relaxed). Similarly, a coiled spring which is com-
pressed under pressure has a tendency to release the tension by
springing back toward its original state.

In tonal music, because of the acoustical phenomenon of the
overtone series certain harmonic structures tend to move to other
very specific harmonic structures. Thus, in tonality, the dominant
seventh chord has a structural tendency to resolve to the tonic chord.
In the popular musical phrase to which we associate the words,
"Shave and a haircut, two bits," if we hear the melody played or
sing it only as far as "Shave and a haircut, two–," we have a tendency
to resolve the tension, which that musical phrase generates, by adding the final note (associated with the word "bits").

To take an example from ordinary conversation, if I ask you a
question such as, "How are you?" the structural tendency is to answer the question. This is because the structure of a question sets
up a tension, and the answer to the question resolves that tension.
This is known as an antecedent-consequential phrase; it is the most
natural phrasing found in language.

Tension strives for resolution. And structural tendencies consist
of tensions arising from the structure, which strive for resolution by
moving along the path of least resistance.

CONFLICT RESOLUTION

Another simple example of a tension seeking resolution is hunger. Thus if you are hungry (tension), the tendency is for you to take action designed to resolve the tension, namely, to eat. Schematically, I put it this way:

TENSION	RESOLUTION
hungry	eat

However, if you are currently overweight, you may choose to go on a diet designed to bring you to a desirable weight. This sets up a separate system of tension resolution. If you are overweight (tension), the tendency is for you to take action designed to resolve the tension, namely, not to eat. Schematically:

TENSION	RESOLUTION
overweight	not eat

You cannot simultaneously resolve both tensions; that is, you cannot eat and not eat at the same time. Schematically, this is quite clear:

TENSION	RESOLUTION
hungry	eat
overweight	not eat

If you attempt to resolve one system, you deny the other and increase the tension in it. If you don't eat, you grow more and more hungry, which increases the tension in the hungry/eat system. Usually, the path of least resistance in this system is to eat, and so the more you don't eat in an attempt to lose weight, the more the structural tendency is for you to eat and hence *gain* weight.

When we look at this sequence of events from a structural viewpoint, that is, when we look at the underlying structure tying those events together, the actions are clearly seen to be a product of structural causality, and their meaning seems quite different from what was intended.

On the level of appearance, people like dieters seem to be taking action to achieve what they ultimately want to see happen, such as losing weight. On the level of structure, however, their actions are designed to resolve a structural conflict. Because of the nature of the structure in play, while they may temporarily lose weight, the path of least resistance will eventually lead them to regain the weight they lost and, thus, move away from the result they want.

Since things are not always what they appear to be, it is often quite difficult for people to know what is really going on.

Actions taken to help or solve a structural conflict often play directly into the dysfunctional nature of the conflict. They also reinforce the underlying structure, and ultimately lead to an experience of powerlessness.

On the other hand, if you eat until your hunger is satisfied, you become more overweight, which increases the tension in the overweight/not-eat system. Here, the path of least resistance is not to eat, and therefore the more you eat, the more the structural tendency is for you not to eat.

One reason dieting is often unsuccessful is that it becomes merely a strategy designed to overpower the structural tendencies in place. What happens, however, is that as one part of the system is manipulated or stretched by the strategy of dieting, the other system (the desire to eat because of hunger) compensates by increasing its dominance. As you put pressure on one part of a system, the rest of the system pushes back. In System Dynamics this is called "compensating feedback."

Mutually exclusive points of resolution are not resolvable, either simultaneously or sequentially. Instead, they set up what I call *structural conflict*. Structural conflict may be defined as *two or more systems seeking resolution where the points of resolution are mutually exclusive.*

Structural conflict operates at a completely different level from that which is colloquially thought of as emotional conflict. Emotional conflict operates primarily at the level of feelings, and is experienced in such forms as anxiety, confusion, frustration, or contradictory emotions such as love and hate for the same person. Structural conflict operates at the deeper, life-orientation level; it may give rise to these emotions or to a wide range of other emotions, from inner peace, lightness, and overwhelming joy, to apathy, heaviness, depression and great sorrow.

[33]

ATTEMPTING TO RESOLVE THE UNRESOLVABLE

There is also a structural tendency to attempt to resolve a structural conflict. It is natural to continue trying to resolve a structural conflict even though the conflict is not resolvable. Many people assume that if something is designed to do something, it will in fact do it. But this is not always true.

In the early days of aviation, many machines were designed to fly which never got off the ground. You may have seen old newsreels of one such machine with its many layers of wings swiftly moving down the runway only to collapse before takeoff with some wings falling off and others falling in upon the machine's body. Another such device had wings mechanically flapping like a bird. While the machine may have amused the designer's friends who had come to watch, it never amazed them as it sat stationary on the runway furiously bouncing and flapping its wings.

Although those machines were designed to fly, there was something innate in the structural makeup of their design that made flight impossible.

Action may be taken which is designed to resolve structural conflict. A predominant structure we often see is unresolvable conflict, and the actions people take are predominantly actions designed to resolve the conflict. The fact that the structural conflict is not resolvable does not mean that the action taken is not designed to resolve it.

For the last five years of their twelve-year marriage, Mary's husband John has not been involved in their relationship. When at home his major activities are eating, sleeping, and watching television. He avoids conversations with Mary and never wants to go anywhere with her. Mary often badgers John about his lack of interest in going out with her and other friends. At least once a week she complains that he is a "stick in the mud" and cares only about his work, not about people. Mary also invites John to go with her to parties, movies, and church events, but John always refuses. Mary is making a number of attempts to involve John in her world, but each time she reaches out to John, he shows no interest.

Mary's actions are taken as an attempt to resolve her conflict. (The conflict is partly based on her simultaneous desire to be involved in her marriage and to be free of it.) But because of the nature of their relationship, the attempts Mary makes to involve John always fail.

[34]

People sometimes take actions which are futile, that is, which have no chance of succeeding. Often it appears that people in a structural conflict are taking action designed to help them achieve what they want; but because of the structure in play, they merely rock back and forth between two points of resolution which are mutually exclusive. A person in a rocking chair has the impression of moving without actually going anywhere.

A CLASSIC CONFLICT STRUCTURE

In the lives of people in the reactive-responsive orientation, there is a basic configuration which is made up of structural conflict plus action designed to overcome it.

The classic conflict structure involves the desire for a certain result and simultaneously a dominant belief which says it is impossible for you to achieve that result.

Suppose you want to have a loving, nurturing relationship and you also have a dominant belief that you cannot have what you want. Because these two elements create structural tendencies toward points of resolution which are mutually exclusive, structural conflict will exist, whether or not you recognize the conflict.

Furthermore, the closer you get to successfully achieving the loving, nurturing relationship, the more the structure compensates by pulling you in the opposite direction.

Figuratively, in this situation, it is as if you were standing in the middle of a room with two giant rubber bands looped around your waist, one firmly attached to the wall in front of you, the other to the wall behind you. Imagine that the wall in front of you represents the pull of the loving, nurturing relationship you desire, and the wall behind represents the pull of your dominant belief that you are incapable of having what you want.

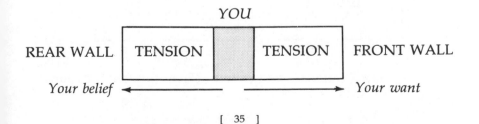

As you move forward toward what you want and the tension created by the rubber band in front of you decreases, the tension created by the rubber band behind you increases. So the closer you get to your desired result, the greater the force pulling you in the opposite direction.

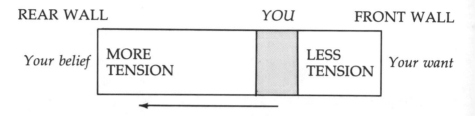

At a certain point, the path of least resistance is for you to move backward. In other words, the easiest thing for you to do at that point is somehow to undermine the loving relationship.

It is not that you are out to sabotage yourself. It is not that there is something deeply, psychologically rooted in you which obsessively forces you to destroy what you want. It is simply that the structure in play has, as the path of least resistance at this point, you not having what you want.

However, your desire to have what you want does not go away. As you are being pulled backward by your dominant belief and the tension is being resolved in favor of not having the relationship, the rubber band attached to the front wall begins exerting its pull forward more strongly, and the longing to have a loving, nurturing relationship increases. In fact, the closer you get to the rear wall, the greater the force pulling you in the opposite direction, toward the desire for a loving relationship.

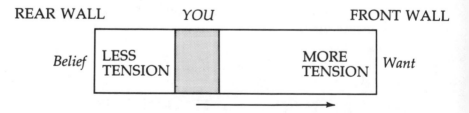

This pattern can play itself over and over throughout your life.

ATTEMPTING TO RID YOURSELF
OF A DOMINANT BELIEF

Often, when people discover the existence of a structural conflict like this in their lives, their first tendency is to try to solve it.

The most obvious approach is to attempt to rid yourself of the belief that you can't have what you want. In theory this approach sounds plausible. But in fact it is unsound.

If you desire to rid yourself of the dominant belief that you can't have what you want, merely substitute the "desire to rid yourself of the belief" in place of the "desire for a loving, nurturing relationship" in the situation we have just described.

Imagine yourself back in the room again with the two rubber bands around your waist, this time the front wall representing your "desire to rid yourself of your dominant belief" and the back wall, as before, representing your dominant belief that you cannot have what you want. The same pattern will play itself out; namely, you will be pulled now toward one wall, now toward the other indefinitely. The attempt to rid yourself of the dominant belief fails.

Furthermore, the very attempt to rid yourself of this dominant belief reinforces the dominant belief, because you have gone after something and discovered again that you can't have what you want.

Some other common dominant beliefs in structural conflict are as follows:

> I am powerless.
> I need to control myself, or I will go crazy.
> I don't have the capacity.
> I am incapable.
> I am not good enough.
> I need to be perfect, and I am not.
> I am not worthy.
> I cannot trust myself, others or the world.

In that the nature of this conflict is structural, *it is only by changing the underlying structure that any real and lasting change can occur.* However, the attempt to change the structure from within the reactive-responsive orientation will not work. Because of the structure in play, the path of least resistance leads to futile actions; actions which are destined to relieve the conflict, but ironically only entrench the conflict further.

CHAPTER 5

EMOTIONAL CONFLICT

The reason that people keep trying to solve structural conflict arises from yet another conflict, this time an emotional one. When most people first discover the nature of the structural conflicts that exist within them they experience conflict on an emotional or feeling level. The usual feelings surrounding this conflict are frustration, powerlessness, anger, fear, resentment, and general discomfort.

There comes a moment when dieters discover that they are stuck in an unresolvable structural conflict, stuck on the see-saw between gaining and losing weight. When they realize that they are likely to remain on this see-saw for the rest of their lives, some grow angry and resentful, others grow terrified and anxious, still others grow depressed and feel powerless. Such feelings are quite uncomfortable. No one likes to live with them for very long.

At this point, many people take strong action, such as joining a dieter support group or deciding to use greater willpower than ever before in remaining faithful to a diet program. Others renew their promises, and assert to their friends and family that "this time things will be different."

What happens when they join the dieter support group, make promises, or vow to succeed, is that some of their anger, anxiety, depression, and feelings of powerlessness begin to recede, and they feel better–at least for a time.

This is the usual pattern of actions and feelings when people experience conflict on an emotional level.

On the level of appearance, such persons seem to be taking action to find out how to be more effective and to overcome what seems to be their problem (being overweight). What is really going on, however, is that they are in an emotional conflict and trying to resolve it. That is, they are experiencing discomfort and are taking action designed to make them feel better. They may indeed resolve their emotional conflict, at least for a time, but the structural conflict (about being overweight) remains.

Many people enter self-help programs apparently to grow and reach for more in their lives. But what is often happening structurally, beneath the surface, is that their action in joining the self-help program is an attempt to restore emotional stability and "solve" themselves as if they were a problem.

Because Jane was generally dissatisfied about her life, including a job she did not like and a relationship that was shaky, she decided to take yoga classes. During the first months, Jane began to feel a sense of renewal and vitality, which she attributed to the yoga classes. After a period of time, her relationship showed no improvement and her job situation became worse than before. She began to feel more powerless than ever, and she felt disillusioned about the influence of the yoga classes on her personal well-being, even though physically she was stronger than before.

Jane originally took the classes in order to help her take charge of her life. Temporarily, she experienced less conflict; but then, as the attempt to improve areas of dissatisfaction in her life had failed, she experienced more conflict. Jane's attempt to make changes in her life came out of a reactive-responsive orientation. No matter what actions or processes she tried from within that orientation, the structural tendency was for them not to succeed.

One of the major forms structural conflict assumes is action taken designed to reduce unwanted emotional experiences. Often the emotional experiences people have around structural conflict are subtle or reach only a low level of intensity, because the people have developed a life-long strategy of avoiding emotional discomfort by means of a pre-emptive strike. That is, they have learned to take action designed to avoid discomfort before it happens. Over a period of years, this pre-emptive strategy of avoiding emotional discomfort becomes a habit. Most often, such people do not have direct awareness of their discomfort because the pre-emptive strike habitually precludes the full intensity of the discomfort from manifesting itself. This is an important point, because it is often difficult to see such

[40]

an avoidance pattern when it is covert. Pre-emptive action is often so habitual that it is no longer a consciously designed strategy.

This habit leads to a set of values in which one of the highest is the value of feeling secure, stable, certain, and unthreatened. Thus, feelings become a standard of measurement of how one is doing in life. For such people, no matter what is actually taking place, if they are feeling uncomfortable, they think they are not doing well.

FEELINGS AS A STANDARD OF MEASUREMENT

In the 1950's and before, it was socially expected for people to bury and suppress their feelings, to the extreme that some parents would not easily or often tell their children that they loved them. Instead, they would try to show love in other ways, for example, by being firm, gruff or teasing, in a manner reminiscent of John Wayne playing a romantic lead in one of his films.

In reaction to this exaggerated suppression of emotional expression, the 1960's gave birth to the "Love Generation" for whom the new social norm was to emote.

When feelings are denied and/or buried, the assumption is that feelings are so important, powerful, and dominant as a force that they ought to be hidden, certainly from others and sometimes even from oneself. On the other hand, when feelings are viewed as the single most important criterion in life, then they are seen as powerful and treated as measurements of truth, to be acted upon whenever they surface. Both extremes are similar in that they both use feelings as a standard of measurement.

Most often, people who glorify feelings have the notion that feelings are steeped in deeply important and significant human urges and events. The various growth movements of the 1970's designed to help people "get in touch with their feelings" gave the impression that when you are in touch with your feelings, something important is occurring of transcendental magnitude.

The fact is that the more you use your emotional feelings as a barometer in your life, the more you are subject to the transitory whims of how you happen to feel at any moment.

For people who have been suppressing their emotions during

their entire adult life, the discovery that they actually have feelings might seem revelatory. Often such people then spend years in pursuit of feelings and their sources, with the result that they become more and more subject to the changing weather of their emotions.

THE POWER IN YOUR LIFE

If your emotions become the dominant factor in your life, the power in your life becomes "how I happen to feel," not "what I truly want."

In contrast, if the power in your life lies in what you choose, you are reunited with your real human power, and the way you happen to feel becomes subordinate to what is actually more important to you.

The truth about feelings is that sometimes you feel good and sometimes you don't. Your emotional state is in constant flux. In real mastery of your life, your commitment is to doing always what is important to do, independent of any emotional experience.

In real mastery, there is no suppression of emotion. There is direct recognition of the emotional state. However, there is no need and no temptation to pander to one's transitory emotional states, because such pandering is a form of self-indulgence which inhibits direct creation.

Among professional musicians, it is often said that the difference between an amateur and a professional is this: amateurs play well when they feel good and when they are in the mood; professionals play well no matter how they feel or no matter what their mood. The point is not that professionals suppress their emotions, but rather that they are not ruled by them. When professionals are creating music, their emotions are important but they remain subordinate to the senior force of the creation of music.

When the importance of feelings is exaggerated, an additional victim is intuition, an important dimension in mastery of one's own creativity. Those who glorify emotions inhibit the natural organic intuitive perception which is easily available to every individual. This glorification is often done in the very name of intuitive perception. But feelings and intuition are two distinct and separate realms of human experience.

[42]

Let no one willfully misunderstand me by assuming I am against feelings. In my view, when feelings exist, it is good to recognize their existence. They are also an important part of the human experience. On the other hand, I am in favor of individuals being able to manifest what is highest in them. More specifically, I am in favor of you being able to be free, healthy, and true to yourself. And the shift from a reactive-responsive orientation to the orientation of the creative changes the relationship that emotional weather has in the scheme of things.

When you make a shift from a reactive-responsive orientation to the orientation of the creative, feelings take on a new meaning. They move from being content to being coloration. The standard of measurement in life shifts from emotional states to what is truly important and most worthy of you as a human being on this planet in this historic period. Your true satisfaction and fulfillment come from nothing short of this.

As one of the greatest scientists of the nineteenth century, Louis Pasteur, said in the midst of a barrage of emotional mockery coming at him from traditionalist academicians, "A man of science may hope for what may be said of him in the future, but he cannot stop to think of the insults—or the compliments—of his own day."

When his friends asked him what he intended to do in the face of these slanderous attacks, he replied simply, "Remain patient—and remain here." He then pursued the project for four more years until he had diagnosed the disease he was investigating, charted the symptoms, and eliminated the trouble.

When I speak of reaching for the highest and living in accordance with what is most truly worthy of you, I am not speaking about overachieving or the superficial Western notion of "accomplishment." Rather I am speaking, as with Louis Pasteur, of being true to yourself and true to your purpose in life.

The reactive-responsive orientation has such built-in structural limitations that it is impossible for you to be a master of your life-building process from that orientation. In a sense, "You can't get there from here."

First, you must go somewhere else.

CHAPTER 6

THE ORIENTATION
OF THE CREATIVE

CREATION EXPRESSING ITSELF

In the orientation of the creative, a fundamentally separate and distinct structure is in play from that in the reactive-responsive orientation.

In the reactive-responsive structure, the path of least resistance is directed toward responding instinctively or appropriately to circumstantial stimuli.

In the orientation of the creative, the path of least resistance is directed toward chosen results.

The image I have when I think of the reactive-responsive orientation is of a person reacting or responding to life as it seems to unfold step by step along the way.

The image I have when I picture the creative orientation is of a person bringing forth something from nothing. I see an inner creation expressing itself outwardly in reality–not merely rearranging what is already there, but manifesting itself with original spontaneity. In the creative orientation, what the creative person creates is something that never existed before.

There was a time when automobiles, telephones, television sets, solar reflectors, and space shuttles did not exist and were not even envisioned.

There was a time when rock music, atonal music, or even classical music did not exist and were not even thought of.

Two hundred years ago the fields of sociology, anthropology, biochemistry, paleontology, and nuclear physics did not exist. Today they do.

[44]

During the last few decades, people have created new dances, new modes of painting, new clothing styles, new fabrics, new ways of understanding the mind, new theories of emotion, new businesses, and new ways of doing business, which never existed before. They all came out of the creative energies of individuals and groups of people.

When composers create, they begin with a blank sheet of music manuscript paper. When artists paint they begin with an empty canvas. It is sometimes difficult for us to think that something new can actually be created, something that did not exist before.

I often hear people assert, "There is really nothing new" or "Everything that is now created has been done before." I usually ask them if anything like Beethoven's *Grosso Fugue, Opus 133*, existed before he wrote it.

Certainly, the string quartet for whom Beethoven composed the fugue had never seen anything like it. In fact, they said that it was unplayable and impossible to listen to, with all of its "random dissonances" and extreme voice-crossings. So Beethoven withdrew the piece and, in place of it, provided the musicians with a tamer work.

When the musicians first saw the *Grosso Fugue*, they thought that old Beethoven had lost his stability, but Beethoven viewed his composition from a different perspective. "I write this music for a future time," he said. Today, most string quartets include the *Grosso Fugue* in their standard repertoire.

The arts and sciences are filled with example after example of new creations, things which never existed before they were created.

However, many people still prefer to think that there is really nothing new under the sun. The writer D. H. Lawrence believed this, until at the age of forty he discovered how wrong he had been.

> I remember I used to assert, perhaps I even wrote it: Everything that can possibly be painted has been painted, every brushstroke that can possibly be laid on canvas has been laid on. The visual arts are at a dead end. Then suddenly, at the age of forty, I begin painting myself and am fascinated.
>
> By having a blank canvas, I discovered I could make a picture myself. That is the point, to make a picture on a

blank canvas. And I was forty before I had the real courage
to try. Then it became an orgy, making pictures.

The discovery D. H. Lawrence made that he could create something new released tremendous energy in him. Creativity does that.
It enables you to bring forth something new.

One of the most important results you can bring into the world
is *the you that you really want to be*. What happens to the blank canvas
is in the hands of the artist. *What you really want to be is for the most
part in your hands*.

When you shift to the orientation of the creative, you firmly
place the authority for the quality and direction of your life where it
belongs: in your own hands. You establish a new bond between you
as creator and reality as your field of creation. The result is a reuniting
with the power of the individual and a renewal of the human spirit.

THE SECRET OF THE CREATIVE PROCESS

A common mistake people make when first entering the orientation of the creative is to seek to "find out" what they want as if it
were a deeply hidden treasure to be discovered and revealed.

They are looking in the wrong direction. Creating what you want
is not a revelatory process, nor is "what you want" something to be
discovered.

If not by revelation or discovery, then how do you derive the
"what" in the question "What do I want?"

The answer to this question is a profound secret of the creative
process.

The answer to this question is known, either rationally or in-
tuitively, by those who are actively involved in creating.

The answer to this question permeates all creative acts, from
creating your life the way you want it to be, to designing the latest
technological advances in computer science.

Our educational tradition unfortunately has had a tendency to
belittle the power and significance of this secret. And yet, once you
begin to use it, new creative power and flexibility are available to
you.

How do you create the "what" in "What do I want?"

YOU MAKE IT UP!!

Please do not miss the point. This is truly a remarkable insight into the deeper nature of the creative orientation. For when you master that orientation, you make up the results you want to create and then you bring them to full manifestation.

Years ago, I consulted with an engineering group in a high tech organization. When I mentioned to the engineers this insight about the creative process, at first they looked at each other with knowing grins. Then one engineer after another said, "That's exactly what we do. We make up what we create." One of them added, "But then we have to write technical articles explaining how we made it up in such a way that it doesn't seem made up!"

MAKING THINGS UP

Creative people know they make up what they create. But there is a strange prejudice in society about the notion of people making things up. One reason is that making things up is not characteristic of the reactive-responsive orientation upon which so much of present society is based. Since the reactive-response orientation relies so heavily on rationale and justification, to simply say "I made it up" seems almost heretical.

Imagine a high school student coming to the history teacher and saying, "I made up a new theory about why the Civil War happened." Or another student coming to the English teacher and saying, "I made up a new kind of poetry." Or another saying to the mathematics teacher, "I am making up a new way of finding the square root of any number." Or another saying to the chemistry teacher, "I'm making up a new process to separate the rare earth metals."

There may be some teachers who would encourage such students to remain actively involved in creating something new. But many would simply tell the students to continue doing things the way they were told to. True creativity is not usually encouraged.

But the fact is that Albert Einstein made up the theory of relativity, Marie Curie made up the theory of radioactivity, Thomas Edison made up the light bulb, Mary Cassatt made up the painting "The Bath," Anton Webern made up the "Six Bagatelles for String Quartet," Emily Dickinson made up the poem, "Because I Could Not Stop for

[47]

Death," Ilya Prigogine made up the theory of dissipative structures, Joni Mitchell made up the song "Court and Spark," Harriet Tubman made up the "underground railway," and the founders of the nation made up the United States of America.

It is common to focus only on the story of how it came to pass that someone made something up. But it is important to realize that, no matter what the stories may be, the creator creates at the moment of making things up. The composer Arnold Schoenberg was asked if he ever heard his music perfectly performed. He replied, "Yes, when I first conceived it."

The clearer you are that as a creator you simply make things up, the freer and more able you will be to make up results consistent with what you truly want to create. Again, the image of a master of the creative process bringing forth something from nothing hints at the great power which permeates the act of making things up.

FOCUS ON THE RESULT

In the creative orientation, the most powerful question you can ask yourself is, "What do I want?" At any time and in any situation–regardless of the circumstances–you can always ask and answer that question.

The question, "What do I want?" is really a question about results. Perhaps a more precise way of asking that question is, "What result do I want to create?"

The question, "How do I get what I want?" is a question about process, not result. As an initial question, it is quite limiting. If you ask the question, "How do I get what I want?" before you ask, "What result do I want to create?", you are limited to results which are directly related to what you already know how to do or can conceive of doing.

In 1878, when Thomas Edison decided to create the electric light, it was already well-known that electricity could produce light. The task before Edison was to find a material which would not burn out and instantly consume itself. He began by reading everything that had been written on the subject, and it is reported that he filled two hundred notebooks with jottings and diagrams. All the scientists before him had followed a certain process: They looked for substances that would reduce resistance to the electric current, but they had found none that would produce an electric light. Instead of following the same process, and limiting himself to producing results he already knew about, Edison tried the opposite: he looked for substances that would increase resistance to the electric current. After testing countless resistant materials, he settled on a carbonized element and placed it in a vacuum bulb, thereby creating the familiar incandescent light bulb.

By keeping his focus on the result he wanted to create–an electric light–Edison felt free to let the process occur in whatever way might bring a successful result.

One of the world's greatest architects, Frank Lloyd Wright, was the creator of Organic Architecture. In designing a house, Wright first looked at the result he wanted to create: for him, it was a sense of interior space for living. In his view, a house was not simply a set of boxes within boxes, with rooms sealed off and connected to other rooms only by doors in partitions and dark halls, but primarily a space in which to live. With his focus on living space as the result he wanted, Wright was open to new possibilities in design, ones that never occurred to most of his fellow architects who were still designing houses by rearranging sets of boxes. In Wright's houses, for the first time, the kitchen became an attractive feature, living and dining area became unified, floor spaces became living spaces, terraces and balconies allowed the outside and inside of the house to flow into each other, floor-to-ceiling windows invited daylight to flood the interior, and low-pitched roofs with wide overhangs created a sense of spaciousness.

As Wright stayed focused on the results he wanted to create, the "how" of obtaining those results developed organically. He did not limit the way of achieving those results to standard procedures.

If you ask the "how" question before the "what" question, all you can ever hope to create are variations of what you already have.

Artists have a clear sense of this need to focus on the result they want. Speaking to young writers, Gertrude Stein once said, "You have to know what you want to get. But when you know that, let it take you. And if it seems to take you off the track, don't hold back, because perhaps that is instinctively where you want to be. And if you hold back and try to be always where you have been before, you will go dry."

[49]

When the process comes first, the process itself will limit the actions you will be able to take and thereby limit the possibilities of what can be created.

As the artist Chuck Close has said, "You can give the same recipe to ten cooks, and some make it come alive, and some make a flat souffle. A system doesn't guarantee anything."

Pablo Picasso, as a mature artist speaking to young painters, encouraged them to let go of tried and true processes and be open to finding their own unique way of creating the results they want.

> With the exception of some painters who are opening new horizons to painting, the youth of today do not know anymore where to go. Instead of taking up our researches in order to react sharply against us, they apply themselves to reanimating the past. Yet the world is open before us, everything is still to be done, and not to be done over again. Why hang on hopelessly to everything that has fulfilled its promise? There are kilometers of paintings in the manner of; but it is rare to see a young man working in his own way.
>
> Is there some notion abroad that man must repeat himself? To repeat is to go against the laws of the spirit, its forward motion.

Premature focus on the process will limit and inhibit your effectiveness.

The educational system does not focus on the results you as a student want in your life. Instead, it promotes the notion that what you should learn is process. You should learn how to do mathematics and construct grammatical sentences. You should learn how to write research papers and do laboratory experiments in biology, you should learn how to draw, to speak in public, to read musical notation, perhaps even to write a poem or two. You should learn how to run a computer and a word processor, and you should learn some crafts skills in shop courses or some household skills in home economics courses. The assumption is that as you become fluent in these processes, the results you want in your life will take care of themselves. Consequently, the question, "What do you want in your life?" is hardly ever asked.

True, for their first ten or twelve years, children are asked, "What do you want to be when you grow up?" But the children's answers are usually discounted unless they happen to follow in the footsteps of one of the parents. Similarly, people often ask adolescents, "What do you want to do when you get out of school?" Usually, even though that question is asked, the young people have had no educational experience of the creative process. From their vantage point, what the game of life looks like is choosing from among alternatives proposed by adults.

In the educational system, aptitude is often substituted for vision. For many, a great tragedy is doing well in certain aptitude tests in secondary school, because the traditional view of guidance counseling is to help students find out what they are good at and help them design careers around their aptitude. Many have mindlessly followed advice coming out of that mentality and become physicians, lawyers, engineers, accountants, nurses, chemists, artists and musicians, only to discover to their dismay, twenty or thirty years later, that they never really cared about what may now be the only field or profession they know. A major part of their life was spent developing what they happened to have an aptitude for at age fifteen.

I know several members of the Boston Symphony Orchestra who are bored being symphony musicians, yet their whole life revolves around the investment they have in staying where they are. One very great musician said to me, "I don't like playing in the symphony, but it's all I know how to do."

ORGANICALLY FORMED PROCESSES

In the creative orientation, when you answer the question, "What do I want to create?" it is not clear whether what you want is possible. Yet throughout the history of the world many results have been created which seemed impossible at the time they were conceived.

Before the creation of anesthesia, physicians were convinced that painless surgery was impossible. In 1839, Dr. Alfred Velpeau said, "The abolishment of pain in surgery is a chimera. It is absurd to go on seeking it today. 'Knife' and 'pain' are two words in surgery that must forever be associated in the consciousness of the patient. To this compulsory combination we shall have to adjust ourselves."

Before the creation of the airplane, many scientists were convinced that flight was impossible. Simon Newcomb, a well-known astronomer, was convinced he had logically proven this impossibility. He wrote, "The demonstration that no possible combination of known substances, known forms of machinery, and known forms of force can be united in a practical machine by which man shall fly long distances through the air, seems to the writer as complete as it is possible for the demonstration of any physical fact to be." Ironically, Newcomb made this statement in 1903–the year the Wright Brothers made their first flights at Kitty Hawk.

Many scientists were convinced that the atom could not be split, nor could an atomic bomb be created. In speaking to President Truman in 1945, Admiral William D. Leahy commented on the United States' atomic bomb program. "That is the biggest fool thing we have ever done," he said. "That bomb will never go off, and I speak as an expert in explosives."

Napoleon was convinced that the idea of a steam engine was impossible and told its inventor, Robert Fulton, so. "What, sir!" exclaimed Napoleon, "you would make a ship sail against the wind and currents by lighting a bonfire under her decks? I pray you excuse me. I have no time to listen to such nonsense."

Once a vision is clear, processes organically form which lead to the accomplishment of that vision. This means that, in the creative orientation, process is invented along the way.

A common rule of thumb in life is to have a formula about how things should work, so that if you learn the formula, you will always know what to do. From a reactive-responsive orientation, this notion is very appealing because with such a formula you would hypothetically be prepared to respond appropriately to any situation. Unfortunately, at best, this would prepare you for situations which are predictable and familiar. Your mastery of those situations would be similar to that of a well-trained mouse in a maze.

From the orientation of the creative, on the other hand, the only rule of thumb about process is not to have a rule of thumb. The process should always serve the result. And since a new result might require a completely original process, limiting yourself to preconceived notions of what processes are available can be fatal to spontaneity.

As painter Jack Beal put it:

I have purposely tried to keep myself relatively ignorant on the subject of color . . . I have tried to keep my color on an intuitive level . . . I have tried not to learn what warm and cool means or what the primary colors are . . . I know some of these principles because you can't help but learn, but I try to let my color be as spontaneous as possible to the subject I'm painting.

It was said of Frank Lloyd Wright that he was never a slave to patterns, not even to those he himself developed.

It is best to allow processes to form organically from within the vision of the result. It is unwise to be in a position in which the way a result can happen is limited by any given process; for at the time the vision is conceived, the actual way it will come about is always unknown to you, even if you have a hunch about it.

A NEW STRUCTURE

The life experiences you now have are, in part, a natural outcome of the structures you have previously established in your life. As we saw before, any approach to life that seeks to overcome past limiting patterns will not work.

Rather than overcoming such limiting patterns, you may establish new and effective ones in which the most natural structural tendencies are toward a fulfilling and satisfying life.

As you establish new structures, outcomes which in the past may have seemed elusive and impossible to create can now be created easily, organically, and quite often effortlessly.

In the last several decades, the computer industry has had a remarkable record of creating the impossible. Today's inexpensive personal computers do things that only a mainframe could do a few years ago. Alan Kay, Atari Computers' current chief scientist said that the new products the industry's visionaries will come up with tomorrow cannot even be imagined today. "The best way to predict the future," said Kay, "is to invent it."

This shift in orientation from the reactive-responsive to the creative requires a new structure to be in play. This new structure I call *structural tension*.

CHAPTER 7

STRUCTURAL TENSION

THE REALM OF STRUCTURE

When I use the term structural tension, I am not referring to the emotional experience of anxiety, physiological or psychological stress, or conflict. I am referring rather to the realm of structure. In structural tension a force is mobilized which helps propel you toward chosen results.

This force is generated from the natural movement of tension toward resolution. As structural tension moves toward structural resolution, energy is released. As you master the principle of structural tension, you are able to generate and release energy which becomes available for direct use in bringing forth what you choose to create.

CREATING STRUCTURAL TENSION

Structural tension requires two components.

The first is to know the result you want; I call this component *vision*.

The second is to know what you now have; I call this component *current reality*. By the term current reality I am not describing some ultimate, absolute philosophical notion of what is real, but rather an adequate and functional description of what events currently seem to be occurring.

The difference or discrepancy between what you have (current reality) and the result you want (vision) creates structural tension.

[54]

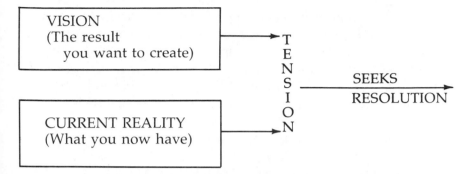

The discrepancy between current reality and vision is to be *cultivated*, not avoided. This discrepancy is of major importance in using structural tension properly.

RESOLVING STRUCTURAL TENSION

Structural tension may be resolved in either of two ways. It may be resolved through a change in current reality, so that your outward circumstances come to correspond more closely with your vision. In this case structural tension is resolved by you having what you want.

For years, Bill wanted a Mercedes sports car. Even though with his salary and other financial obligations he knew he could not currently afford to buy one, it was still the car he wanted. Every week, he would check the automobile section of the newspaper studying the availability and cost of the Mercedes sports car he wanted. One day, Bill heard about someone in his company being transferred, who was selling the kind of sports car Bill had in mind. Although he presumed he would not be able to afford the car, he talked to the man selling it. Because the man wanted to sell the car quickly, he was willing to sell it for much less than the current market price–for an amount which happened to be in Bill's price range. In Bill's case, the structural tension was resolved in favor of having the kind of car he wanted.

On the other hand, the tension may be resolved through a change in your vision, so that you alter the result you want to correspond more closely with what you now have.

Like Bill, Steve had always wanted to drive a sports car, but with his job he also could not afford to own one. Instead, he drove an inexpensive, second-hand sub-compact that ran faithfully in all kinds of weather and got good mileage. For some time, Steve was aware of the discrepancy between his vision of a shiny sports car and the current reality of his gray sub-compact. At first, he felt frustrated at not having what he really wanted. But he began to think about all the good points of his present car, and he invented reasons why he probably would not want the sports car after all. Eventually, he convinced himself he was better off with current reality and gave up the idea of wanting a sports car.

By not maintaining your vision of the result you truly want, you reduce structural tension.

If you have an intolerance for not being where you want to be, that is, an intolerance for discrepancy between current reality and your vision, you will tend to translate that discrepancy into psychological discomfort, experiencing feelings such as anxiety and frustration.

The path of least resistance out of psychological discomfort created by this intolerance leads you to take action designed to reduce the discomfort and restore comfort. Steve's action was to convince himself that he was better off with his present car. He discovered that the action that would reduce this discomfort fastest would be to alter or lower his vision in the direction of current reality.

When you alter or lower your vision to reduce discomfort, structural tension is weakened because you are no longer aspiring to what you truly want, but rather to a compromise.

The life-spirit and energy which contribute to the mastery of the creative process can never be fully engaged by a commitment to a compromise.

Although Steve's desire for a sports car may not be an example of his highest aspirations in life, the way he compromised his vision in that case was an example of a pattern in his life of settling for less than the highest, because of his intolerance for not having what he wants.

Weakening structural tension will relieve, temporarily and superficially, the discomfort of your intolerance for the discrepancy. But this will also set up a pattern of powerlessness, and what becomes powerful is your discomfort. Your compromise is designed precisely to relieve that discomfort. It is a little like selling your soul to get the heat off.

You are also reinforcing your low threshold of tolerance (that point of discomfort beyond which you are unwilling to go). Whenever your threshold is reached, you will be ready to compromise in order to relieve the discomfort.

IGNORING CURRENT REALITY

Another common way of dealing with intolerance of the discrepancy between current reality and vision is to continue holding the vision while attempting to ignore current reality. This is the path of the idle dreamer who exists in an ivory tower wishing for life or the world to be different but unable to effect any real and lasting change.

Here are included all those people who dreamed of writing the great novel, opening a world-famous restaurant, climbing Mt. Everest, sailing alone across the Atlantic, adopting a foreign orphan child, helping bring fairness and justice to the oppressed or converting the masses to enlightenment–and yet have not lifted a finger to accomplish it. Many of these people wait to be discovered; others wait for an invitation to change the world; others wish for their "sincerity" and dreams to be recognized by the right people.

Idle dreamers have given true visionaries a bad name. True visionaries do not ignore current reality, they appreciate it for exactly what it is.

Current reality sometimes contains circumstances which are unwanted, unpleasant, and often painful. Seeing current reality may also at times produce anxiety and discomfort. People who explore their lives in depth, perhaps with the aid of psychotherapy or counseling, often discover that they are more self-centered, jealous, greedy, anxious, dependent, controlling, and authoritarian than they ever thought they were. Therapeutically, this new awareness is very helpful for human growth and development. However, people often deliberately ignore some of the most obvious aspects of current reality– the smoker who ignores his cough, the teacher who ignores the disrespect of her students, the boss who ignores his employees' inefficiency, the woman who ignores her husband's abuse of her. Since new awareness of what they have been ignoring might contradict many of their assumptions and notions about their own identity, they tend to perceive current reality as a threat to that identity.

[57]

In addition, current reality might suggest that there are ways in which you need to change. You may need to become less controlling and less manipulative in your relationships, take more initiative and be more adventurous in your job, develop new skills and become more assertive in your life in general. Such change may be disruptive and uncertain for you and, therefore, unwanted. A natural reactive-responsive avoidance strategy in this case would be actively to ignore any aspects of current reality which might challenge your view of life.

Since ignoring current reality is action taken designed to relieve discomfort, this action is not directed toward realizing your vision. Rather, it is a reaction directed away from current reality. What becomes dominant is an underlying structural conflict. Action is then taken–action designed to attempt to resolve the underlying structural conflict, which is of course unresolvable. What is lost is the great power of structural tension.

MAINTAINING STRUCTURAL TENSION

In the orientation of the creative, the discrepancy between current reality and vision is an important dynamic, for out of that discrepancy the natural play of structural forces can be fully engaged and mobilized to bring about the results you want.

For the moment, think of yourself as a master of the universal play of forces, and that by virtue of your mastery you are always able to work *with* the forces rather than oppose them. In this view of mastery, which is the orientation of the creative, there is never any resistance to overcome, no breakthroughs to make, no problems to solve, no obstacles to conquer, because the structures which exist in reality most naturally, organically, and powerfully contribute to your full development.

Current reality is not your enemy, but your foundation and starting point. It contains latent within it perfect structures, as the structure of an acorn has latent within itself the potential of becoming an oak tree. When you work within these structures rather than against them, you enable yourself to move along the path of least resistance toward the fulfillment of your life purpose.

CHAPTER 8

CURRENT REALITY

HOW TO KNOW YOUR CURRENT REALITY

First and foremost, develop the habit of making observations about the circumstances in which you find yourself. Cultivate observing the obvious. For instance, "It's ten o'clock in the evening. I'm hungry. My partner and I are getting along. I like what's happening now, but I realize I don't like what's going on at work. What I don't like is that the job I have is boring." Etc.

In observing your current reality, avoid any explanations of why something might be so. If you find yourself explaining to yourself or to others how things got to be the way they are, you are describing not current reality but rather your theory of the origins of current reality.

"Did you take out the garbage?"

"Well, I just came in the door."

"But, did you take out the garbage?"

"I was going to, but the phone rang, and I had to answer it. Then I needed to go out quickly and get something."

"Oh, so you didn't take out the garbage?"

"I can't be always taking out the garbage. What do you expect from me?"

Current reality actually includes the garbage which had not been taken out. One person is attempting to establish this fact of current reality, while the other is trying to explain how current reality got to be the way it is.

When you first begin to make observations about your current circumstances, it is extremely tempting to discover what might be causing them to be the way they are. This is a blind alley. Usually such explanations are designed to reduce any discomfort arising from actually seeing how things are.

When observing current reality, include what you now have that you like and would like to have continue. Include also what you have that you don't like and would not like to have continue. Here, someone might say, "I like my relationship with my partner and would like it to continue" and "I don't like this backache I now have and would not like it to continue."

When looking at what you do not like, avoid any attempt to solve or resolve it. Someone might say, "I don't like my job. Well, I should quit then, shouldn't I?" or "Mary always talks too much. Of course, she's always been a compulsive talker, so I just let her talk without paying any attention to her." These are attempts to solve or resolve what you do not like about current reality. Such attempts create a smokescreen, making current reality harder to observe.

On the other hand, avoid exaggerating or minimizing what you see. To say, "Mary was talking so much that I thought I'd go deaf just from listening to her" would be an exaggeration. To say, "Once in awhile, Mary talks a little more than most people, but it doesn't really get in the way" would be to minimize. A description of this situation, neither exaggerated nor minimized, might be, "Mary talks more than I would like to listen to her."

It takes practice to report the facts without giving an editorial. Pay attention to what you are telling yourself. Make sure you avoid coloring or distorting your description to create an effect. You are looking for an adequate and accurate description of what is presently occurring in your circumstances. As Robert Frost said, "Anything more than the truth would have seemed too weak."

You may have an investment in not seeing current reality fully for a number of reasons. One reason, as we have seen, is that current reality might make you look bad. Another reason is that it might make others look bad, and you feel the need to protect them. Thirdly, current reality might be threatening because you "should not" be where you actually are.

In relationships, a common disorienting factor is partners finding that the nature of their relationship is different from what they thought it was. For example, a woman finds that her husband is not making the same assumptions about the future as she is, or a man in a company assumes he is being relied upon for his opinion only to find that his advice is frequently disregarded. When people have an investment in being where they thought they were, they find it more difficult to see clearly and easily what is truly going on.

A fourth reason you may have for not seeing a full view of current reality is that current reality would deny how you have represented yourself to yourself and others. One friend of mine chronically represents herself as incapable and inadequate. Over the years, she has developed a certain investment in this portrayal of herself. Actually, the current reality is that she is an enormously talented, gifted, and capable person.

OVERVALUING APPEARANCES

In our culture, undue emphasis has been placed on appearances. Here, I am referring not only to physical appearances, but to all the ways we attempt to represent ourselves to others. Looking good has become a national way of life. Every year thousands of businesses go bankrupt slowly and inconspicuously as the people in those organizations hide current reality from each other in an attempt to "look good."

Journalism has also succumbed to the temptation to celebrate appearances, particularly since the Kennedy administration. A popular word during those years, "charisma," became a new standard of measurement. Since then, every president and presidential candidate has been measured against Kennedy's charisma. For many journalists, it has become easier to measure appearance and style rather than substance. One reason journalists favor Ronald Reagan and disliked Jimmy Carter was because of appearances. Ronald Reagan creates a good image; Jimmy Carter didn't. Under these criteria, we may wonder how great presidents such as Abraham Lincoln, John Adams or even Thomas Jefferson would have fared in a test of appearance.

In any age, when appearances become overly valued substance is lost. Much of contemporary life as reflected in television, film, and popular song encourages people to look like movie actors, television celebrities, or rock stars. What becomes supremely important is how one looks to peers. Under these circumstances being true to yourself is hardly encouraged, especially if it results in you not appearing to be what you "should" be or not doing what you "should" be doing.

Another disadvantage of appearance being highly valued is that it distracts us from seeing what is real. What is actually occurring in current reality occurs independently of our perception of it. Current reality does not disappear just because it may go unrecognized. It is always an essential element in the structure, and therefore has much more influence than appearances. Current reality does not go away. Moreover, it ultimately finds expression, and its expression has much more impact than appearances.

Things are exactly what they are, and no amount of hype or propaganda alters what they are–as many recording companies, film studios, and book publishers have discovered.

A man who heads a large service organization called his senior staff together for an in-depth organizational meeting. He had noticed, from time to time, a temptation among his staff to create policy designed solely to promote the organization's image. At the meeting, the leader established, clearly and definitively, a new standard for the company: that no action be taken and no policy set which in any way established "appearance" as a value. What was important to him was what was real. His wisdom lay in knowing that essence communicates directly and "truth will out." Since that time, the organization has doubled in growth every year.

In the reactive-responsive orientation appearance is important. In the orientation of the creative appearance is incidental; what is important is the result. It matters little what process Rembrandt used to paint his masterpieces, except to scholars and artists studying his technique. What does matter is the painting itself, the result. It matters little to us that Mozart composed his music at an unbelievably effortless speed, often as fast as his pen could write, while Beethoven often struggled and labored over each phrase. What matters is the greatness of the music itself.

A friend of mine related to me what her ski instructor told her when she was just learning. He said, "If it feels right, it's probably wrong. And if it feels wrong, it's probably right." He was trying to prevent her using "it feels right" as a standard of measurement. Instead, he was encouraging something different. He knew that for her to succeed as a skier she would have to position her body in ways that were new and unfamiliar, which in the beginning would feel wrong to her.

If you use your feelings as a standard of measurement, you will always gravitate toward what is familiar. If you are creating something new, something that has never existed before, at least in your life, then the path from here (current reality) to there (your vision, or result) by its very nature will be and feel unfamiliar.

DESIRE TO KNOW CURRENT REALITY

Why would you want to know current reality?

Only from the knowledge of current reality can you build a foundation for the future. You can get to New York City from Boston by traveling generally southward for about two hundred miles. However, if your actual starting point is Chicago, and you think you are currently in Boston, you may travel generally southward for about two hundred miles but you will end up far from New York City. It is important to know your starting point in order to be able to go where you want to go.

Another reason for wanting to know current reality is that structural tension, the dominant structure in play in the creative orientation, cannot exist without a clear view of current reality.

Furthermore, your sanity and psychological balance are influenced by how you relate to current reality. One major difference between creative people and schizophrenics is in their ability to define current reality. Creative people successfully define current reality; schizophrenics do not.

The ability to define current reality is a skill which can be developed. As you work with current reality over a period of time your ability will increase. As you improve, you develop a kind of inner strength and inner security.

There is a deeper wisdom within you which knows the important role current reality plays in the entire scheme of things. Current reality is never really a threat. The ignorant do not experience bliss. You can build your life on the sure foundation of current reality and be supported by it.

On the other hand, to glorify current reality is to render it useless.

Many growth workshops tend to promote a glorified view of current reality. The idea promoted in them is that all you can have is what you presently have, and all you can choose is what you already have.

This glorification imposes a fixed view of how things are. When your view of current reality becomes fixed, it is no longer current. Develop the habit of looking continually at current reality to see how it now is, and do not assume that it now is the same way it was the last time you happened to look.

THE HABIT OF KNOWING CURRENT REALITY

Most people have the habit of ignoring selected parts of current reality. Popular psychology calls these "blind spots." In developing the habit of seeing current reality, it is important to include looking into those areas which might be habitually missed. In order to develop this habit, *consciously pay attention to current reality on a regular basis*. Practice frequently and objectively describing to yourself what your current reality is.

I might say, "I am sitting in a room with white walls and an oriental rug on the floor. On one side is a blue couch with white polka dots, on the other are two wicker chairs and a wicker love seat. The room is filled with plants of various sizes."

Descriptions like these are good exercises in practicing objective observation. *Continue to practice describing to yourself what is going on around you in all kinds of situations, including human interactions, until this way of seeing becomes automaic.*

MOMENTS OF POWER

It is important also to make a point of looking at current reality whenever life is not going the way you want. It is common for most people to see the times when things are not going the way they want as moments of powerlessness. I see these moments as among the most powerful in your life. *In the creative orientation, times when things are not to your liking can directly lead to times when things are very much to your liking.*

Honestly looking at current reality in order to create structural tension is not to be confused with so-called positive thinking, that is, telling yourself you like something you really do not like, or telling yourself that things are going well when they really are not, or encouraging yourself to be positive in the face of adversity. Nor is what I am suggesting a sort of blind optimism, hoping that present negative circumstances will somehow turn out well in the end.

You never want to be in a position of lying to yourself about anything. If you do not like current reality, part of this current reality is that you do not like it.

Liking current reality on the one hand, and appreciating its significance as a powerful moment in the creative process on the other, are two different matters. With more direct experience of the orientation of the creative, you will begin to appreciate even those moments in which current reality seems disadvantageous, because you will know the power and significance of such moments and where they can lead.

While developing the habit of seeing current reality is an essential element in the creative orientation, it is not enough. You also need to know where you want to go and the results you want to achieve. In the creative orientation, this is called vision.

CHAPTER 9

VISION

QUALITIES OF VISION

The word vision has many uses. Some people use it to refer to clair-voyant experience, others use it to refer to a visualization process. I use vision in the context of structural tension.

By vision I mean the inner crystallization of the result that you want to create, so that the result is conceptually specific and tangible in your imagination–so tangible and so specific, in fact, that you would recognize the manifestation of the result if it occurred.

If you had a vision of owning a ten-room home in a wooded area close to a lake, you could easily recognize the result if it occurred. Similarly, you could easily recognize a job which utilizes and expands your talents and abilities, a relationship which is loving, interesting, and mutually supportive, a vegetable garden of large, ripe, juicy tomatoes, crisp lettuce, and large, tender ears of corn, and so on. In each case you could recognize the manifestation of the vision if it occurred.

Artists and musicians use inner vision in crystallizing the result they want to create.

For the composer, a vision usually takes the form not of a sudden flash of music, but of a certain result that the composer wants to realize as perfectly as possible.

Roger Sessions, the American composer, speaking of how Bee-thoven's musical vision affected his compositional process, wrote, "When this perfect realization was attained, there could have been no hesitation–rather a flash of recognition that this was exactly what he wanted."

"This vision of the whole," Sessions went on to say, "assumes an ever more preponderant role, and appears more and more to be the essential act of creation."

The vision of the whole is an essential element in all of the creative arts. In a conversation with artists, Picasso described how the original vision of a painting affects the final result.

> It would be very interesting to record photographically, not the stages of a painting, but its metamorphoses. One would see perhaps by what course a mind finds its way toward the crystallization of its dream. But what is really very serious is to see that the picture does not change basically, that the initial vision remains almost intact in spite of appearance.

Vision has power, for in vision you can easily reach beyond the ordinary to the extraordinary. You have only to imagine yourself in the nineteenth century–before indoor plumbing and electricity, before refrigeration and air conditioning, before radio and television, before jet flight and mass transportation, before power tools and permapress clothing, before telephones and superglue–to see the extraordinariness in the vision of inventors and technicians.

Vision also has a magic quality. I define magic as seeing the results without seeing the entire process leading to those results. Roger Sessions observes that the composer is not so much conscious of his ideas and processes as he creates but is led on by his vision. "Very often," Sessions explains, "he is unaware of his exact processes of thought till he is through with them; extremely often the completed work is incomprehensible to him immediately after it is finished." It is as if the composer had been led to the result by his inner eye of vision. Many creative people express this sense of surprise and awe at their own creations.

The inner eye of vision can see what isn't yet there, can reach beyond present circumstances, and can see what, up to that point, has never been there. It truly is an incredible human faculty that is able to see beyond the present and the past, and from the unknown conceive something not hitherto in existence.

The great twentieth century composer Karlheinz Stockhausen wrote, "We need to close our eyes for a while and listen. There is always something unheard of in the air."

Even though the airplane was not invented until the twentieth century, Leonardo da Vinci's vision, almost five hundred years before, led him to sketch a machine designed to fly.

For the composer and painter, vision may have to do with creating new works of art. For the inventor, vision may have to do with creating newer and better machines, electronic apparatus, or appliances.

But the structures of creativity may be used for more than creating new works of art or technology. They may be used to help you create the life you want. You can use them to see what is not yet present in your life, to reach beyond today's circumstances, to conceive a new and more effective "self" for your life that has not yet come into existence.

Vision has to do with inner seeing; it emanates from imagination. Not all things imagined are vision, but all vision comes from imagination. Anyone who can speak a language uses imagination. Words are a combination of sounds (spoken language) or a combination of symbols on a page (written language) which can come alive only by the use of imagination. There is nothing intrinsic to the four letters that spell the word "tree" or the sound of the word "tree" spoken aloud that has anything to do with an actual tree. It is only through our imagination that we make the association between an actual tree and the related symbols of communication.

If you can read this sentence, you have all the imagination you need to create the life you want.

IMAGINATION AND REALITY

Imagination is not a threat to reality. If you are a highly imaginative person, your imagination in no way limits your ability to discern what current reality is, and in some ways it might even contribute to that ability. Conversely, reality is not a threat to imagination. Seeing current reality does not limit your ability to use imagination; in fact, it might even contribute to that ability. Since creativity and imagination are natural to human beings, it is unnatural to limit them the way most people have been trained to do.

Traditional education often attempts to limit and control imagination, in part because of the fear that children will not be able to recognize and "cope" with reality if they have a well-developed imagination.

Some educators talk as if imagination would lead students to see unreality–what really isn't there–rather than realizing that imagination can lead them to seeing *reality yet to be created*. Although "creativity" is praised with lip service, some educators tend not to know about or practice using imagination in their own lives, which makes it very difficult for them to teach imagination to their students.

In many cases, people have so stifled their ability to use their imagination that they assume they cannot imagine their life being significantly different from the way it is now. Because they cannot imagine their lives being what they want, they continue to live their lives in ways they do not want.

Although imagination by itself is not enough to develop the ability to create what you want, you are limited in your creativity by that which you can imagine.

When my son Ivan was four years old, I was talking to him on the phone and I asked him to tell me what I was wearing. "I don't know, Daddy," he replied. "I can't see you."

"Well tell me, Ivan," I said, "what can you see in your imagination?"

"Oh, in my imagination!" he replied. "In my imagination I can see everything."

He then proceeded to describe accurately the clothes I was wearing, including the colors of each item.

In your imagination you can see everything, including how you would like your life to be.

VISION AND DESIRE

Desire means wanting something. The things you desire may be very specific. You may want such things as a short story accepted by *The Atlantic Monthly*, a cure for leukemia, a place on the Olympic swimming team, or a trip to Ireland and Scotland.

Your desires may be more general ones such as good health, an uninhibited sex life, a business started, peace in the world, or scientific cooperation among nations. Most desires take these more generic and nonspecific forms, and that's where vision becomes really crucial in the creative process.

Vision is a crystallization of what you want to create. Vision takes your generalized desire and shapes it into a clear and definable result. Vision takes your basic desire to make an impact on the world and specifies it in the image of a college education, a book published, or a project for the city. Vision takes your basic desire for a happy life and specifies it in the image of a farm in the mountains, stable and loving relationships, or a fulfilling job with enjoyable colleagues. Vision takes your basic desire to have your life in order and specifies it in the image of organized closets and drawers in your room, a will made out, a balanced checkbook, or a calendar marked with all the birthdays of family, relatives and friends.

Vision is not arbitrary, for what you want is not arbitrary. For years, you may have been suppressing or not admitting to yourself what you most deeply and truly wanted. But what you want is still in your consciousness.

Trying to rid yourself of desire is futile for a number of reasons. First of all, your desire to rid yourself of desire becomes a new desire. Second, since ridding yourself of desire is often associated with certain spiritual traditions and a certain desired result such as spiritual fulfillment or spiritual enlightenment, there is an implicit desire built into the process of trying to get rid of desires. Finally, since we as humans operate in a plane of existence in which structures have tendencies, it is impossible to live outside of tendencies, some of which are desires. The underlying dynamic of space, time, and substance is movement; and the way that movement is directed is along the path of least resistance. Thus, to try to rid yourself of desire is as futile as attempting to hold back the ocean tides. Not only is it contrary to nature, it cannot be done.

An almost opposite ineffectual approach to desire is to surround your desires with great fervor, vitality, and intensity. Thus instead of making a simple choice to have your desire, you might write it as an affirmation a thousand times, or you might spend ten minutes each day breathing deeply and forcefully while you think of what you desire, or you might cover the walls of your room with pictures of what you desire. Such ritual behavior is a form of self-manipulation that produces a number of unwanted effects. First, by taking such extraordinary measures, you are training yourself not to listen to your simple, everyday choices. Secondly, you are giving yourself the message that the creative power you need to produce results can only be evoked by using extraordinary measures. Finally, over a period of time, the ritual approach reinforces the notion that there is no power in what you simply want and choose, but only in the extraordinary means. Ultimately, this approach results in reinforcing your deep experience of powerlessness.

In the orientation of the creative, you do not have to cut yourself off from what you desire, nor do you have to jump up and down in extraordinary behaviors to get what you want. The power to *create* what you desire is yours. To release that power you have only to make simple choices. How do you begin? By telling yourself the truth about what you really want.

INHIBITING THE VISION

In order to conceive of what you truly want to create, you must separate what you want from what you think is possible. In 1903, when Orville and Wilbur Wright were building their first airplane, the rest of the scientific and technical world were asserting the impossibility of a heavier-than-air machine sustaining itself in flight. What the Wright brothers wanted was certainly not based on what seemed possible. But they held to their vision.

If you find yourself limiting what you want based on what seems possible to you, you are censoring the process and inhibiting your vision.

If you are not admitting to yourself what you want simply because it does not seem possible for you to have it, what you are actually doing is misrepresenting the truth to yourself.

Lie detectors measure physiological stress. When you lie to yourself or misrepresent the truth in any way, you increase the stress on your body. After years of misrepresenting your true wants, the increasing stress can lead to health problems. You never want to be in a position of lying to yourself, for in some way such lying always breaks down your relationship with yourself, creates stress, and represents the truth as potentially dangerous and threatening.

Once I was leading a workshop for The Easter Seal Foundation.

The group with whom I was working were all in some way suffering from lung ailments such as emphysema, lung cancer, and asthma. In one section of the workshop, the objective was for participants to practice separating what they really wanted from what they thought was possible.

One elderly woman was having particular trouble with the exercise.

"Remember, the exercise is to separate what you want from what you think is possible," I said to her. "So, what do you want?"

"I can't say," she replied. "It really *isn't* possible."

"Well, yes," I said, "but for the moment, don't consider whether or not what you want is possible."

"I can't say what I want because I can never have it."

"I can tell you what you want," I said.

"You can?"

"Sure," I replied. "What you want is good health."

"But I can never have it."

"But isn't that what you want?"

"But I can never have it," she insisted.

"Well," I began, "If I were a magic genie and could wave a wand and give you perfect health, would you take it?"

She paused for a moment, and quietly said, "Yes."

"If you would take it," I added, "you must want it. Furthermore, even if it doesn't seem at all possible to you–even if it's *NOT* possible– the real truth is that you want perfect health."

"Yes," she said. "That's so."

"So, now tell yourself the truth about what you want," I said. "It's never wrong to tell yourself the truth, even though you think it's not possible."

She paused. Then, looking down at the floor, she said quietly, "The truth is I want to be healthy."

"What just happened to you when you said that?" I asked.

"I don't understand this," she replied, looking surprised. "I feel physically lighter, as if a weight has been lifted off my shoulders. I feel clearer. It's almost as if there is an energy flowing through me now."

Whether or not her illness persisted, she no longer had to bear the additional burden of feeling obligated to misrepresent to herself the truth about her desire for health. Certainly, the additional stress she was placing on herself by denying what she wanted was not helpful.

There are enough well-known instances of people being able to overcome great health obstacles, partly by holding a clear vision of the result they wanted, that it would be presumptuous to say miraculous cures are impossible. "Babe" Didrikson Zaharias, Olympic sports figure and professional golfer crippled by sickness, was told she would never walk or play golf again; she held the vision of herself playing professional golf, and she lived to play tournament golf for many years. Expert physicians held no hope for Helen Keller, left blind and deaf by an illness in infancy, to ever take her place as a contributing member of society. But her teacher, Anne Sullivan, held the vision of a Helen who could communicate, be responsible, acquire an education, and serve society in unique ways.

Extraordinary changes like these are far less likely to happen as long as you lie to yourself or misrepresent the truth about what you really want.

The phenomenon that the woman described of being physically lighter (a weight lifted off her shoulders) and feeling energy flowing through her is a very common experience when you begin to tell yourself the truth about what you want.

WHAT TRULY MATTERS

There is a difference between what you truly want (that for which you would invest your life spirit) and some fantasy you may have. Before actually reporting to themselves what they want, some people often assume that what they want is great wealth, good looks, power, or something else that advertising or their culture tells them they should want.

Do not confuse idle wishes, fantasies, and the convincing "sell" of a television commercial with that which you most deeply want. They are very different.

The more you realize that what you truly want really matters, the more selective you become about what you want. You recognize the importance of your deepest wants, and less important ones take a secondary place.

As you reunite with your power to create, most likely you will discover that what truly matters to you is worthy of you—for example, health, freedom, justice, and being true to yourself.

For most people, when they begin clearly to know what is important to them, they discover what might be called their "natural goodness." As Robert Frost put it, not some "tenderer-than-thou, collectivistic, regimenting love with which the modern world is being swept," but an authentic and practical caring for higher values, both of the individual and for the planet.

PROCESS OR RESULT

In crystallizing a vision, the result you want to create is important. But how do you know whether what you want is a result or a process?

If you want something because you think it will lead to something else you want, you are focusing on process. If you say you want money, but actually you want money because of what it would bring you, perhaps economic freedom, financial security, a new car, or a home—you are focusing on money as a process. In this example, the result you really want is what the money is designed to bring you.

A result is independent of what brought it to you, and independent of that to which it might lead. And *in shaping a vision the result you want to create is what is important.*

THE COMPLETE RESULT

In conceiving what you want, be sure to describe the complete result. This means the whole picture, including the circumstances surrounding its manifestation.

Too often, in creating a vision people assume they can focus on specific results but cannot focus on the total effect those results will have. A major revelation for many is that they can choose not only the specific results they want but also the broader concomitants of those results.

In one workshop a woman said she wanted to be more spontaneous. When I asked her if she had any doubts about having more spontaneity, she thought for a moment and said, "Yes, if I were spontaneous, I'm afraid people wouldn't like me."

I asked her, "Do you want people to like you?"

She quickly replied, "Oh, yes. I want people to like me."

"So you want two things," I said. "You want to be spontaneous and you want people to like you. Is that more accurately the result you want?"

Without hesitation she said, "Why yes! That's exactly what I want. I never thought of it that way."

When creating a vision of what you want, it is important to be in the habit of conceiving the whole picture, not just a small part of it. Therefore, include in your vision what you want to create, the circumstances and qualities of what you want to create, and the full context in which you want it to appear.

A TEST QUESTION

Once you have identified what you want to create, ask yourself this question: "If I could have that result, would I take it?"

If the answer is "Yes," then you really want it.

If the answer is "No," then either you don't really want it or you think having that result would bring you some undesirable condition or conditions. If the latter is true, as was the case with the woman who wanted spontaneity, broaden the range of your desired result by addressing those undesirable conditions.

A VISION WORTHY OF YOU

Not all vision is equal. The vision with the most power is the vision that is worthy of you. A common mistake people make when they first shift into the orientation of the creative is to be shy about what they want.

Conceiving what you want is truly an individual act. No one can do it for you, and no one can tell you what to want. But I do encourage you to aspire to what is highest in you and deepest in you.

During the early days of World War II England was, in the eyes of the rest of the world, in its darkest hour. Belgium had surrendered to the Nazis, France had fallen, Russia had apparently aligned with Hitler, and the United States was not yet involved in the war.

Churchill, however, was keeping alive his vision for England. When he faced his Cabinet, he said, "Gentlemen, we are alone. For myself," he added, "I find it extremely exhilarating."

When Germany seemed about to launch its long-threatened invasion of Great Britain, Churchill shared his vision with his fellow-countrymen:

> We shall defend our island, whatever the cost may be. We shall fight on the beaches. We shall fight on the landing grounds. We shall fight on the fields and in the streets. We shall fight in the hills. We shall never surrender.
>
> Let us brace ourselves to do our duties, and so bear ourselves that, if the British Empire and Commonwealth last for a thousand years, men will say, "This was their finest hour."

Churchill was well aware that current reality was asserting that this was England's darkest hour. But he was also in touch with his desire for his country, and he also held fast to his vision, that this was England's finest hour.

His vision helped a battered British military to keep fighting until Russia and the United States had time to organize enough resources and personnel to turn the tide of the war.

The creative genius of Churchill's statesmanship lay in his ability to envision the result he wanted in its fullest expression, and then to hold fast to his vision while remaining in touch with current reality.

Among the leaders of the world, Churchill remains a shining figure in his extraordinary ability to be in touch with current reality. He was often able to see the historic implications of the times in which he was living far more clearly than those around him. In addition, from the beginning of the twentieth century, he continued to shape the vision of many social and international structures.

Most of those who knew Winston Churchill as a boy would never have imagined that he would be capable of such depth and vision.

In the orientation of the creative, most people discover depths in themselves they never knew existed.

THE POWER OF STRUCTURAL TENSION

Structural tension, which is created by the discrepancy between current reality (the way things really are) and vision (what you truly want), is a *senior force* and takes precedence over structural conflict. Since in the creative orientation all structural conflicts which exist in current reality merely become *part* of current reality, in that orientation they do not call for resolution.

You can create important results in your life even though you are currently involved in structural conflict.

Elizabeth has always wanted to run a French restaurant. Elizabeth's current reality includes a typical structural conflict between, on the one hand, her desire to create those things that she wants and, on the other, a dominant belief that she does not have enough capacity to create what she wants.

When Elizabeth was in the reactive-responsive orientation, this structural conflict was a major factor in her life, and she never seemed to have enough time, money, cooperation from other people, and other necessary resources to accomplish what she set out to do. The dominant structure in play at those times always had Elizabeth taking action attempting to resolve her unresolvable structural conflict.

When Elizabeth made the shift to the orientation of the creative, structural tension became the dominant structure in play. Her structural conflict did not go away. She still believed she did not have the necessary capacity to accomplish what she wanted. This structural conflict, however, merely became part of her current reality. Elizabeth was aware of her structural conflict as she was aware of other elements in her current reality.

Elizabeth then chose to create the intimate, French style restaurant she had wanted for many years. This project depended on capacity (resources), for example, money for equipment, a place for the restaurant in a good location, restaurant help and especially a good French chef. In the orientation of the creative, the discrepancy between Elizabeth's belief that she does not generally have enough capacity (as part of her current reality), and the demands for capacity that her vision holds actually contributes to structural tension. This discrepancy also contributes to the full accomplishment of what she wants to create.

Elizabeth is no longer trying to resolve an unresolvable conflict. Rather she is using current reality as a foundation upon which she is building what she wants. In fact, the discrepancy between current reality and her vision directly generates energy to be used in creating what she wants.

When you create structural tension by observing current reality and simultaneously holding the vision of what you want to create, enormous energy and power are generated, because the path of least resistance is to resolve the discrepancy between the two in favor of the vision. As Churchill and the people of England discovered, great changes may occur organically as current reality moves toward the vision. Under such circumstances structural conflict is not an inhibiting force, but actually contributes to the manifestation of the vision. Everything in current reality contributes to structural tension by virtue of being part of the discrepancy.

Furthermore, in the orientation of the creative not only is the discrepancy tolerated, it is actually appreciated. Many studies show that creative people like Winston Churchill, the Wright brothers, and Anne Sullivan have a unique ability to maintain and sustain discrepancy between how things are and how they want them to be.

The force generated by structural tension changes in its nature as it moves through the stages of the creative process. If you are to master the creative process, you will need to master each of the stages in the cycle. The following chapters are designed to help you move toward that mastery.

PART TWO: THE CREATIVE PROCESS

CHAPTER 10

THE CREATIVE CYCLE

THREE STAGES OF CREATION

There are three major stages in the growth and life-building process: germination, assimilation, and completion. Every complete creative process moves through this cycle and always in the same sequence.

Looking at the creative cycle as expressed in the process of human birth, germination occurs at conception; the prime initiating act from which the entire process emanates.

Assimilation, the second distinct stage, is akin to gestation, during which the fetus goes through internal growth and expansion.

Completion, the final stage, occurs when the birth takes place.

This human birth cycle is natural and organic.

It is no surpise that the creative cycle, which is natural and organic, has the same three stages.

GERMINATION

In creating the results you want, germination has a very special energy–energy characteristic of any beginning. You tend to feel this burst of energy when you initiate projects: when you first begin a new diet, when you start a new job, when you first bring home a new piece of stereo equipment, when you meet someone with whom you hit it off well, when you start a new class or workshop, when you first start a new business, when you first buy a house.

Composer Roger Sessions, in an article "The Composer and His

Message," describes germination as "the impulse which sets creation in movement."

The great joy for filmmaker Alfred Hitchcock was in conceiving his films. For months before cameramen, scripts, actors, or other details, were discussed, he thrived on germinational energy, constructing on paper the entire movie, frame by frame. He was fond of saying that filming the movie itself was much less exciting to him than conceiving, writing, and planning it. Hitchcock took special delight in the germinational stage of creation.

During the initial stages excitement, interest, and freshness abound. It is a time for generating action. There can be great insight, realization, enthusiasm, change, and a sense of power. These experiences of germinational energy dissipate over time, often a short time.

Most approaches to human growth and potential focus exclusively on germination. While it is an important and powerful stage, by itself it is not sufficient to produce real and lasting results, for it is only one step in the whole creative process.

ASSIMILATION

A crucial second step is assimilation. Like the gestation period of the human birth cycle, assimilation is the least obvious stage of growth, particularly in its beginning phases.

During this internalizing stage, the result being created is growing organically, developing from within, and calling forth inner resources, and you are taking inner and outer action.

Dot had to write a proposal for a new project, but was not sure just how to organize the material. All the information was in her mind, but she had not yet found a way to express it clearly and insightfully. She mulled it over a while, then went to the watercooler for a drink of water to distract her conscious mind. When she came back to her desk, one section of the proposal began to take shape. Soon another section fell into place. Momentum began to build and, faster than she could write, the rest of the proposal came together in a completed whole. Of course, she had some editing and adjusting to do, but the result essentially manifested itself.

A similar assimilation stage, of shorter or longer duration, occurs when you are learning a new dance, a new foreign language or a new skill.

Whenever you are creating anything, there is always a period of time when the germinal idea is taking root and forming itself. Assimilation is essential if germination is to have any real meaning.

Although artists have difficulty describing assimilation, they are aware of it and of its essential contribution to the creative process. They are in touch with the inner, hidden quality of their activity at this stage.

Roger Sessions describes this second stage as the composer experiences it, calling assimilation 'execution.'

> The process of execution is first of all that of listening inwardly to the music as it shapes itself; of allowing the music to grow; of following both inspiration and conception wherever they may lead. A phrase, a motif, a rhythm, even a chord, may contain within itself, in the composer's imagination, the energy which produces movement. It will lead the composer on, through the force of its own momentum or tension, to other phrases, other motifs, other chords.

In a letter to a friend about how a composition forms itself, Mozart underlined the hidden quality of assimilation, the musical idea forming itself somewhere within, appearing when it is ready, not able to be forced out before its time.

> When I am, as it were, completely myself, entirely alone, and of good cheer—say, travelling in a carriage, or walking after a good meal, or during the night when I cannot sleep; it is on such occasions that my ideas flow best and most abundantly. *Whence* and *how* they come, I know not; nor can I force them. Those ideas that please me I retain in memory, and am accustomed, as I have been told, to hum them to myself. If I continue in this way, it soon occurs to me how I may turn this or that morsel to account, so as to make a good dish of it, that is to say, agreeably to the rules of counterpoint, to the peculiarities of the various instruments, etc.

Or, as Gertrude Stein, talking to artists, graphically described assimilation, "You cannot go into the womb to form the child; it is there and makes itself and comes forth whole—and there it is and you have made it and have felt it, but it has come itself."

The stage of assimilation generates momentum, so that as you move through the creative cycle the path of least resistance is toward the result taking shape, forming itself, becoming an entity.

The famous mathematician Henri Poincare viewed assimilation as work done at an invisible level. For him, the result produced was "a manifest sign of long, subconscious prior work." In an article "Mathematical Creation," Poincare described how important this inner work was and how its momentum eventually moved it into conscious form.

> The role of this subconscious work in mathematical invention appears to me incontestable, and traces of it would be found in other cases where it is less evident. Often when one works at a hard question, nothing good is accomplished at the first attack. Then one takes a rest, longer or shorter, and sits down anew to the work. During the first half-hour, as before, nothing is found, and then all of a sudden the decisive idea presents itself to the mind.
>
> It might be said that the conscious work has been more fruitful because it has been interrupted and the rest has given back to the mind its force and freshness. But it is more probable that this rest has been filled out with subconscious work and that the result of this work has afterward revealed itself to the geometer just as in the cases I have cited. Only the revelation, instead of coming during a walk or a journey, has happened during a period of conscious work, but independently of this work; the conscious work plays at most a role of excitant, as if it were the good stimulating the results already reached during rest, but remaining subconscious, to assume the conscious form.

Poincare described a concrete personal instance of the assimilation process helping make a connection between two apparently unconnected fields of mathematics. It followed a period of intense work "apparently without success."

Disgusted with my failure, I went to spend a few days at the seaside, and thought of something else. One morning, walking on the bluff, the idea came to me, with just the same characteristics of brevity, suddenness and immediate certainty, that the arithmetic transformations of indeterminate ternary quadratic forms were identical with those of non-Euclidean geometry.

The profound result produced by this connection turned out to be the opening of a door into new areas of research in mathematics.

COMPLETION

The third distinct stage of creation is completion, which includes bringing to fruition, manifesting the whole, concluding, finishing, and following through.

Bringing to fulfillment that which you are creating is obviously important. Few people have mastered this stage. Most have not.

All of us know people who do not bring their creative activity to completion: graduate students who need only to write their thesis in order to receive their doctoral degree, but never finish it; entepreneurs who begin businesses, yet somehow never bring them to financial viability; amateur boat builders whose home-made sailboat in the garage just needs the final caulking, but they never quite finish it so that it becomes seaworthy; people who start classes in Tai Chi but, just when they are beginning to acquire a degree of mastery in the art, discontinue it.

It may be said of many that they can snatch defeat out of the very jaws of victory!

Some people feel uncomfortable having what they want. Receiving is an essential phase of completion, and hence of the creative process. As you master the stage of completion, you need to master the ability to receive the fruits of your endeavors.

Just as a composer releases a new composition to the public, so persons who create in other realms release their work to the world. The created result is set free from its creator; it can then be received by its creator.

Cole Porter is said to have experienced this letting go and receiving whenever one of his musicals opened. After the opening, he thought of the work as something outside himself. For him, the completed result possessed an autonomy beyond the intention of the creator. For most artists, creating a work is like giving birth to a child which, when born, assumes a life and identity uniquely its own.

MOVING FORWARD

A certain unique energy is generated in each of the three stages of the creative cycle. That energy helps you move from the stage you are in to the next stage. The energy of germination helps you move to assimilation, the energy of assimilation helps you move to completion, and the energy of completion helps you move to a new germination.

Cole Porter's completed musical inspired him to begin writing another. Henri Poincare's mathematical discoveries at the seashore sent him back to his home in Caen to create new mathematical connections and discoveries. The painter's finished canvas leads him to germinate new ideas for future paintings.

It is the nature of creative energy not to run down, but to increase and multiply itself.

After creating a successful gourmet meal, it's easy for you to create another gourmet meal. After you once grow a successful garden, it is easy for you to plant and grow a garden the next year.

Completion urges you to move forward.

Special energy is present in each of the three stages of the creative cycle. We explore each stage in turn.

CHAPTER 11

GERMINATION
AND CHOICE

MAKING CHOICES

Germination does not consist merely of conceiving what you want
and establishing a direction in which you want to go, but most importantly in activating the seeds of your creation. The way you activate the seeds of your creation is by making choices about the results
you want to create. When you make a choice, you mobilize vast
human energies and resources which otherwise often go untapped.
All too often, people fail to focus their choices upon results and
therefore their choices are ineffective.

AVOIDING EFFECTIVE CHOICE

In the reactive-responsive orientation, there are eight common
ways in which effective choice is avoided or undermined, and by
which the potential power of choice is lost.

Choice by limitation is choosing only what seems possible or reasonable. George wanted to be a doctor. However, his parents and
teachers continually dissuaded him from that life-course because of
the difficulties involved. Although he had the intellectual ability to
pursue a career in medicine, it seemed impossible for him to support
himself financially through medical school, so he eliminated the possibility of becoming a doctor from his aspirations, and only consid-

ered career paths that seemed "reasonable." He became a pharmacist.

If you limit your choices only to what seems possible or reasonable, as George did, you disconnect yourself from what you truly want, and all that is left is a compromise. George never had the same enthusiasm for and attraction to pharmacy as he had for medicine, for the reason we have noted: it is impossible to invest the human spirit in a compromise.

Choice by indirectness means choosing the process instead of the result. Thus some choose to go to college rather than choose to be educated, or they choose to eat health foods rather than choose to be healthy. Because this kind of choice invests undue power in the process, the result is inextricably tied to the process, and the way in which the desired result can occur is limited.

Harriet always thought her problems stemmed from her bad relationship with her father. Over the years she read many books designed to help her "release" her unexpressed anger toward him. She attended several workshops which focused on that process, and pursued various therapeutic approaches which focused on releasing unexpressed emotions. During these sessions, she would sometimes find herself screaming at the top of her lungs, crying her eyes out, making lists of grievances toward her father, conducting imaginary dialogues with him, sharing with groups the story of her and her father. What Harriet actually wanted was to be a whole person. However, the processes she chose were not really what she wanted. She chose them thinking they would bring her what she wanted. Through the pursuit of process, however, Harriet was never able to create the wholeness she sought.

Often people become so involved in processes that the results they truly want are obscured. They then have little chance of getting what they desire. In many cases, they are not even aware of the result they are after.

Choice by elimination typically occurs when a person escalates the conflict in a situation by polarizing differences to a point where they are irreconcilable. For example, after exacerbating an argument in a relationship, one person tells friends, "Things got so bad, I had to leave. I had no choice." The power here is assigned to the situation, and the situation is then manipulated to eliminate any other choice but to break up.

One of the tendencies in modern times is to polarize the political left and right, so that all that remains are two undesirable extremes: tyranny from the right or tyranny from the left. People see themselves as choosing the lesser of two evils. Certainly choice by elimination is what we see happening with tragic consequences in Central America, Northern Ireland, the Near East, and Africa.

Choice by default is the "choice" not to make a choice, so that whatever results happen seem to occur without choice. Because of an inability or unwillingness to choose, the person assigns the power to the situation, and abdicates his or her own power. Refusal to choose cripples the creative process in its earliest stages.

Conditional choice follows the typical formulas: "I will choose this when . . ." or "I will choose this if . . ." Rather than choose directly the result they want, some people impose certain conditions or circumstances upon the result. "I'll be happy when I find the perfect relationship." The implication here is that they will not be happy until they have the perfect relationship, and their choice to be happy is dependent on whether or not they have a perfect relationship. Such persons place the power in certain arbitrary external conditions, and these conditions somehow then are supposed to have the mystical ability to set up an environment which brings satisfaction.

Choice by reaction is the epitome of choice arising out of structural conflict associated with feelings of discomfort. It occurs when persons make choices, not to initiate a creative process, but merely to reduce discomfort. As soon as circumstantial stimuli reach a critical level of discomfort, the person makes a choice which is designed to relieve the discomfort. The power here lies in whatever produces discomfort, and the choice is made solely to eliminate that discomfort.

Society trusts that most people make choices by reaction, so when society does not want people to act in certain ways, it threatens to make life uncomfortable—fines, prison, eviction, humiliation, ostracism and even capital punishment. Choice by reaction is often a "knee-jerk reaction," as when some drivers automatically slow down whenever they see a state policeman.

Choice by consensus is made by finding out what everyone else is willing to recommend and following the results of that poll. Because consensus is often achieved by successful preliminary public relations, the vote at the poll usually turns out to be consistent with what the person actually wants to do. However, since others are giving the advice, it is not by the person's own choice that the person acts but by the will of the group polled.

A woman described her choice by consensus in the following way. "My boss is hard to talk to, and I've been extremely bored lately in my job. I don't feel any support from the rest of the staff. In fact, they all seem to care about things that are completely superficial and unimportant. Meantime, I've just had this new job offer in an exciting organization. The new job seems challenging, involving, and important. And the people with whom I'd be working share my real caring for organizational transformation. What do you think I ought to do? Do you think I ought to quit my job and take the new one?" It is difficult to imagine anyone advising her to stay in the old job. In this example, the public relations activity was quite overt. Usually it is more covert and subtle, but the general strategy is still the same.

Once I knew a man who practiced a variation of choice by consensus. When faced with a decision, he would collect advice and opinions from several people he knew. Then he would follow the advice of those who agreed with what he wanted to do. If it turned out that this choice was not successful, he would go back to the people whose advice he "took" and blame them for his failure.

Choice by adverse possession is based on a hazy metaphysical notion about the nature of the universe. It goes like this: "I have hemorrhoids, therefore I must have chosen them." The notion is that whatever you possess in current reality you have somehow chosen. If you accept this notion as true, you are forced to conclude that some "part of you" outside your awareness has chosen all of the circumstantial stimuli operating in your life, including those you do not "consciously" want. The power in your life then lies in some unknown "part of you" and therefore beyond your reach.

Actually the life experiences you now have are in part a natural outcome of the structures you have previously established in your life. If the path of least resistance produces outcomes you do not like, their causes may be found in the structural makeup in play, rather than in some perverse or unwitting choice you may have made.

The way a person chooses reveals where the power in a situation resides, and how the power is being activated and used. In each of these eight ineffective ways of choosing, characteristic of the reactive-responsive orientation, the power in the situation is abdicated or handed over to something or someone outside the person.

Since one can create only with power and energy, in the orientation of the creative the power in the situation is assumed to be residing in the person creating.

CHOICE IN THE CREATIVE ORIENTATION

In the creative orientation, you consciously choose the results you want to see manifested.

Choosing is deceptively simple, yet it does take practice to do it correctly. As I have mentioned, one way of making a choice incorrectly is to commit yourself to a process rather than to the result you want. Many people engaged in processes designed to bring them specific results have never actually chosen those results, either formally or informally. Some people who eat special health foods, take large doses of vitamin supplements, exercise assiduously, and avoid alcohol, coffee, tobacco, chocolate, bleached flour, and refined sugar have never made the choice to be healthy. People can do all these healthful things and still not make the choice to be healthy.

In many instances, they have chosen a process of doing what is "good for them." But it is as if they are investing all of their energies in the process, hoping the process will bring them to a desirable result. What has happened is that they are committed to the process, and not necessarily to the result.

Formally making the choice to be healthy mobilizes the inner resources of the body. By choosing to be healthy, you set up structural tension. Through this choice you thus focus and release energy, and you then tend to gravitate toward those processes which will be most healthful and helpful to you. When you merely choose a process, structural tension is not established, and energy is not available to complete the creative process.

CHOOSING NEGATIVE RESULTS

Instead of choosing health, some people choose the negative result of "avoiding sickness." When you choose a negative result, structural tension is not established. What you set up is structural conflict.

Certain people who engage in strict diet-and-exercise regimes are not really in favor of health, but rather against getting sick. The focus of their fear is not merely the common cold, but illnesses such as heart attack, cancer, ulcers, hypertension, diabetes, and other diseases which would seriously impair their way of life or threaten their very existence. They follow a strategy of avoidance, emphasizing what they do not want (serious illness or death) rather than what they do want (vitality and life). Their behavior arises out of a structural conflict in which the path of least resistance is to take action designed to attempt to resolve an unresolvable conflict.

This structural conflict, revolving around feelings of discomfort, is a life-versus-death conflict. Because they want to make sure that they survive, i.e., that they do not get seriously ill or die, they keep in mind a negative vision—the vision of themselves at any moment possibly succumbing (getting cancer or having a heart attack). They have thus polarized the conflict. They maintain a high level of pressure at all times because they cannot afford to slide back into illness. Their strategy is to keep themselves in a state of conflict. They may say to themselves, "If I eat sugar and white flour, I'll get cancer and won't live, so I'd better make sure I don't eat food like that. I must remain vigilant." The actions they take, such as eating organically-grown foods and doing exercise, are not focused toward health, but are actually designed to restore the experience of emotional comfort—to reduce the fear and worry they have generated in themselves.

Over a period of time, they establish that they are powerless: that the power lies in the food or exercise, not in themselves; that their life is threatened by eating certain foods and not exercising; that left to their own devices they would be irresponsible, so they need to control themselves by maintaining in their awareness both the potential danger of slacking off in their practices and their irresponsibility about keeping these practices up. What they have is a long-range strategy designed to compensate for their irresponsibility, in a situation in which the power lies in the external circumstances, i.e., in the food they eat.

This self-manipulative structure generalizes itself in many areas of life. It will be the subject of a later chapter (Chapter 18, Conflict Manipulation).

I am not saying that there is anything inherently wrong with eating healthy foods and getting plenty of physical exercise. In the orientation of the creative, once you have consciously made the choice to be healthy, when you are attracted to eating certain foods and following certain forms of exercise you are involved in an organic process. The structural tendency of this organic process is for you to be attracted to those processes that will be particularly beneficial to your health. Those processes might include the usual expected ones, such as health foods and exercise, as well as unexpected ones.

When you try to impose processes on yourself synthetically you may lose touch with your own natural life-rhythms, which may call for you to do very different things as these rhythms change. For example, you may have a policy of eating a fixed diet each day; however, your life-rhythm may call for more protein on one day than on another. Because of your fixed diet, you might miss the foods or nutrition your body requires to enhance your state of health.

WHAT YOU DON'T WANT

Do not make choices about what you *do not* want. Make choices about what you *do* want. A common mistake when beginning to consider what you want is to see only what you do not want.

Knowing what you now have that you do not want can, of course, be useful information, because often the opposite of what you do not want is what you do want. If you do not want your car to keep breaking down, what you do want is a car that consistently runs well. If you do not want to work under boring conditions, what you do want is an interesting and challenging job. If you do not want to argue and fight all the time with your partner, what you do want is the opposite, namely, a loving, supportive, and harmonious relationship.

When you focus large amounts of energy on the problems in your life, it is easy to remain fixated on those problems. At certain times, the only thing that seems important to you is to get the problem to stop being a problem, or to have it go away. Relief from the problem is uppermost in your mind. The more entrenched the problem seems, the harder it may be to separate what you want from what you do not want or from what you think is possible.

Quite often I have spent fifteen minutes or longer simply asking someone the question "What do you want to create?" only to have the person continue to say "I don't want this" or "I don't want that" or "I don't want to have to deal with this" or "I'd like to be rid of that."

Imagine Beethoven trying to create *The Grosso Fugue* (Opus 133 for String Quartet) by using only a list of things he did not want it to be. "I don't want it to be orchestral music. I don't want it to be a piano piece. I don't want it to be like other compositions I've written. I don't want it to be expressionless, etc., etc." As you can see, focusing on what you do not want does not create much of a vision, nor does it generate any germinational energy.

Choices about what you do not want emanate from the reactive-responsive orientation, because the major focus in that orientation is on reacting or responding to what you do not want. Moreover in such a situation what you do not want holds the dominant power.

FORMALLY CHOOSING

In making a choice there are two steps. First, conceive of the results you want, i.e., have a clear vision of what you want to create. Second, formalize the choice by actually saying the words "I choose to have . . ."

It is not important that you say the words aloud, but certainly say them to yourself and also inwardly truly make the choice to have that result. Saying these words is not muttering an incantation with mysterious magical powers. When you make a formal choice, you activate the seeds of germination. You initiate the first stage of the creative cycle.

For many, making such a formal choice seems to be a momentary leap into the unknown, especially if the choice they are making involves something important they have never chosen before. After that moment of uncertainty, however, often come experiences of clarity, energy, and physical lightness. Whether or not you have unusual experiences, when you make a choice in the orientation of the creative you actively set energy in motion in your chosen direction. Choices about results have power.

CHAPTER 12

PRIMARY AND
SECONDARY CHOICE

Three distinct kinds of choices operate as strategic elements in the creative process: primary choice, secondary choice, and fundamental choice. In this chapter, I deal with the first two.

PRIMARY CHOICE

Primary choices are choices about major results. You may make a primary choice to have a good relationship, a meaningful job, a house in which you really feel at home, or a wonderful vacation. You may make a primary choice to create a work of art, to cook a good meal, or to conduct an exciting workshop or meeting.

A primary choice is about some result you want (in itself and for itself), not something that you want because it will lead you to something else–even though it may. A primary choice does not function mainly as a step in a series of steps.

A choice that helps you take a step toward your primary result is called a secondary choice. Thus, you might choose to go shopping (secondary choice) in order to have the ingredients for the meal you want to cook (primary choice).

While a primary choice may also bring other results into being or be a foundation for future results, its major purpose as a choice is to achieve what is being chosen. When an artist paints a painting, the primary choice is for the completed painting itself to exist, rather than for the painting to be a stepping stone in the artist's career, or a way of bringing the artist emotional satisfaction, or a way of earning money. A primary choice is an end unto itself.

If you have a doubt about whether what you want is a result unto itself or part of a process aimed at attaining some other result, you can ask yourself the question: "What is this choice designed to do?"

If it is designed to help achieve something beyond itself, it is part of a process. It is, therefore, not a primary choice but at best a secondary one.

If it is not designed to bring you some further result, then it is a result in and of itself and therefore can be a primary choice.

When I asked my wife Rosalind why she plays the piano, she said, "Because I love to play the piano." This is an example of primary choice.

Even for famous artists at times, their primary choice in creating may be the joy of creating. As Henry Moore, the famous sculptor, once remarked, "And I sometimes draw just for its own enjoyment."

A friend of mine who is a very good cook said to me while preparing dinner for us, "What I like to do is get involved in improvising in the kitchen. Often, like tonight, I don't know exactly what I have in mind for dinner. I like to see what will turn out when I enjoy playing around with the ingredients."

My friend had indeed made a primary choice, which had at least two results. The first was a good meal. He may not have known earlier that evening exactly how this particular meal would end up looking or tasting, but he knew the qualities of a good meal. We could be sure that the first result he created–a good dinner–would successfully match the aesthetic and gustatory criteria of a good meal.

The second result he had in mind was the sheer joy of cooking. This result was like my wife's joy at playing the piano, or like a mountain climber's excitement in scaling a mountain, or like a vacationer's delight lying on a sunny beach. For him, the experience of cooking was an end in itself, independent of the dinner it would produce.

For people in the reactive-responsive orientation it is often difficult to make a primary choice, because emphasis is placed more on the process (how to get where they want to go) than on the result (where they finally want to be). Process itself is seen as the most important activity in their life. I have met people so totally involved in process that they could not conceive of the results they wanted. Instead, all that they could conceive of were process steps which led to other process steps.

"What do you want?" I asked a man during a workshop.

"Well, I want to get in touch with myself," he replied.

"What will you have once you are in touch with yourself?" I asked, trying to help him to focus on the result he wanted.

"Then I can see what holds me back," he replied.

"What will happen once you can see what holds you back?"

"Then I can overcome the way I sabotage myself."

"Once you know that," I asked again, "then what?"

"Then I can stop doing it."

"What will happen when you stop doing it?"

"Well, I don't know," was his reply.

When people who are focused on process are asked where their process is leading them, they often do not see where it might lead, even five or six steps down the line.

At times, people in the reactive-responsive orientation have in mind some vague or implicit results such as "leading a good life" or "being in touch with feelings" or "making a difference." But these results, too, are usually so obscured by process and are so process-dependent that they have no impact on the person's life and no tangible meaning.

Many people these days tell me they want to "make a difference," but when I ask them "What *kind* of difference?" their answers are often nebulous and vague.

It is important to answer that question. After all, Adolf Hitler made a difference. So did Joseph Stalin.

We may assume that the "difference" people usually speak of is not a negative difference. But too often, finding out what they really want to accomplish is like grabbing at smoke.

Because of this vagueness, their chance of making a clear and positive impact on their individual lives or the life of the planet is tremendously limited. It is limited not by lack of commitment, not by lack of altruism, and not by lack of desire to be of service to the planet, but by their failure to make tangible primary choices. When desired results are, at best, implicitly defined, not much can happen, no matter what the depth of commitment, the height of altruism, or the sincerity toward service.

On the other hand, in the orientation of the creative results are not *implicit* but *explicit*. The results in mind are clearly defined. They are so tangible that you would recognize them if you had them. You would recognize a good relationship if you had one, just as you would recognize good relations among nations working together for the benefit of humanity if it were happening. You would recognize a satisfying job if you had one, just as you would recognize worldwide advancement in human endeavor in technological, artistic and social areas if it were happening. You would recognize a good meal if you had one, just as you would recognize food sufficiency for all people of the world if we had it.

In the creative orientation, the dominant activity is creating results. Whether the desired results are an oil painting, a good dessert, or good relations among nations, the person who creates envisions (makes up) the desired results, and brings those results into reality.

AN EXERCISE IN PRIMARY CHOICE

There is tremendous power in knowing what results you designate as primary. Once primary choices are made, you may effectively and naturally rearrange and reorganize your life in ways that help bring those primary choices into reality.

When you formally make a primary choice, germinational energy is generated and new strategic secondary choices become clear and apparent. When you make these strategic secondary choices, you match your actions to the result you want to create, so that each step you take creates a foundation for and builds momentum toward the full realization of the primary choice.

Step 1. Make a list of everything you want, from now through the rest of your life. Include both personal and professional wants. Include what you want in your relationships with others. (Do not include ways specific people should behave. To say, "I want Harry to do such and such" is an attempt to impose your will on Harry. Rather focus on the nature and quality of the relationship you want. Write "I want a relationship which has the following qualities . . ." The relationship you ultimately create may or may not be with Harry.) Also include what you want for the world in general.

Be sure to list only those items that you want. Do not include items that you do *not* want such as "no more war," "no more arguments with my wife" or "no more ulcers." Also do not include items you think you *should* want.

Treat this list as a first draft.

Step 2. Reread your list to make sure it includes all of the major components you want in your life. Add anything you may have forgotten in your original list, and cross off any item that you do not really want.

Step 3. With each item on your list:

> Be in touch with the fact that you want it. Ask yourself the test question, "If I could have that, would I take it?"
>
> If the answer is no, then either cross the item off your list or adjust it so that it is something you want.
>
> If the answer to the test question is yes, formally choose the item.

Step 4. Continue the process until you have chosen every item on your list that you want.

By making these choices, you have taken the first step in the creative process. Conceiving and choosing what you want is an act of germination. As you choose what you want, you release germinational energy which enables you to move in the direction you want to go.

SECONDARY CHOICE

Secondary choices are those which support a primary choice.

Some months ago I decided to have a well-toned body. That was my primary choice. As a secondary choice I signed up for a three-month Nautilus exercise program. There were many other secondary choices I made, even daily, to support my primary choice.

Often during the program I would wake up in the morning and the thought would occur, "I could stay in bed this morning. After all, I've exercised the last few days. I am doing a good job. I don't really need to go in this morning!"

I would then get out of bed and go downstairs in my robe and slippers.

Downstairs, the thought would occur to me, "Now that I'm awake, I can just go to the bathroom and then right back to bed. After all, I don't really need the exercise!"

I would then put on my sweatsuit and sneakers.

Once dressed for my workout, the thought would occur, "Now that I'm awake and dressed, I could lounge around and read some more of that book I like so well, and have a very pleasant morning!"

By this time, I would have put on my jacket and walked out my front door.

As soon as I was in the car, the thought would occur, "Now that I am in the car–This is great!–I can drive down to get some croissants!"

I would then drive to the Nautilus gym.

Usually by this time thoughts of avoiding exercise would have temporarily disappeared. However, about two or three exercise routines before the end of the series, the thought would occur, "I've done a good job! I've certainly done enough for the day! I don't have to finish all the exercises in the series!"

I would then proceed to finish the last few exercises.

This is an example of making a series of secondary choices to support the primary choice. I was able to choose to get out of bed when it would have been more convenient to have stayed in bed; get dressed, when it would have been more convenient to go back to bed; leave the house, when it would have been more convenient to have stayed at home; drive to the gym, when it would have been more convenient to drive to the bakery; and complete the entire series of exercises, when it would have been more convenient to cut them short. Each step along the way I was easily able to make these secondary choices, because I had clearly made the primary choice.

At no point along the way did I experience a sense of loss or think that I was giving up anything. Most of the thoughts that occurred were descriptions of what was possible. It is true, I could have stayed in bed, could have stayed home reading, could have gone for croissants, and could have cut the exercises short. All of those were choices I could have made.

At each point of decision, however, I was able to see clearly what mattered to me more. At no point was there a need to argue with myself, and at no point did I argue with myself. What mattered to me more at each point along the way was my primary choice to have a well-toned body. Each of the secondary choices I made–to get up, to go to the gym, to complete the exercises—was made easily and without hesitation *because it directly supported my primary choice.*

Not all secondary choices are as easily accomplished as getting out of bed or getting dressed. For persons who have chosen to be professional musicians or athletes, secondary choices may involve years of practice. In the creative orientation, once you know your primary choice, whatever secondary choices need to be made in order to achieve the primary choice become clear along the way and easy to make. They become the most obvious course of action to take. Athletes and musicians practice long hours not out of duty, obligation, or any other form of self-manipulation, but because they make secondary choices consistent with their primary choice to be able to perform music or excel in sports.

MUTUALLY EXCLUSIVE WANTS

If you wake up tired one workday morning and you want to stay in bed but your job requires that you be at work at a particular time, how do you make the choice of whether to stay in bed or get up and go to work?

In such a situation, there are two things that you want, but having one of them prohibits having the other. You cannot both remain in bed and be at work on time.

Once you know what your primary choice is, you will easily know what to do.

If your job is your primary choice, then the secondary choice will be the choice that supports the primary one, which is to get out of bed, get dressed, and go to work.

Some people are confused when two things they want are mutually exclusive. They feel stuck, unable to choose. As a consequence, they often do not make a real choice. Instead they get up and go to work as automatons or out of guilt, fear of punishment or loss. Unless they make a real choice in such situations they will always feel leftover reluctance and perhaps even resentment, no matter which alternative they end up doing. They may physically go to work, but spend some or all of their time there mentally still in bed, resenting the imposition of their work schedule.

In the reactive-responsive orientation, a conflict of this kind is usually experienced as a dilemma, and therefore unresolvable. The two alternatives are seen as being of equal value and importance. In choosing one or the other, reactive-responsive people always experience loss and a degree of powerlessness. In their view, circumstances are forcing them to give up something they want.

In the orientation of the creative, *you as creator determine the hierarchy of importance among results*. Then you choose what is primary. This enables you always to be in the powerful position of inventing along the way the course of action which most effectively supports the result you value more (your primary choice). Instead of experiencing a sense of loss and powerlessness about the things you want but can't have, you are always choosing the things you want most. The things you want less become subordinate to your more important wants.

Furthermore, as you make secondary choices in order to support your primary choice, the primary choice becomes even more clearly defined as an important result and, therefore, can be even more easily created.

It became easier for me to create a well-toned body by making the various secondary choices I did along the way, for with each additional secondary choice I clearly defined a well-toned body as primary for me.

In making such secondary choices, it never seems as though you are giving up anything. When you make secondary choices–when you actually make the choice supporting what is primary–the experience you have is of doing what you truly want. It is empowering.

CHAPTER 13

FUNDAMENTAL CHOICE

FUNDAMENTAL CHOICE AS A FOUNDATION

A fundamental choice is a foundation upon which primary and secondary choices rest.

If you have never made the fundamental choice to be a nonsmoker, then no matter what system you try to help you quit smoking, it will not succeed. You may try hypnosis, or aversion therapy, smoke-ending programs, gradual elimination, or cold turkey. None of these processes will successfully help you become a nonsmoker, if you have not fundamentally chosen to be a nonsmoker.

On the other hand, if you have made the fundamental choice to be a nonsmoker, just about any system to stop smoking will work for you. Furthermore, after making the fundamental choice, you will tend to be particularly attracted to those systems which will work best for you, because by using them you will most easily get the job done.

A fundamental choice is a choice in which you commit yourself to a basic life-orientation or a basic state of being. Being a nonsmoker is a basic state of being, very different from the state of being of a smoker who is trying to quit smoking.

THE ACTIVE POWER OF FUNDAMENTAL CHOICE

When I first began working with people in the area of human endeavor and creativity, I was struck by the fact that some people in my DMA classes would easily create the results they wanted, while others in the same classes would not. For years I wondered what made the essential difference, since often those who were the most successful were not the ones who originally seemed most likely to succeed.

When I discovered fundamental choice, I realized that those who were most successful were persons who had made the fundamental choice to have the life they wanted, and were consequently using what they were learning in order to create that life.

Those who had not made that fundamental choice had a very different orientation toward their own growth and development. Rather than making it their business to see that they succeeded in having the life they wanted, they passively let circumstances dictate what happened. They hoped somehow that the circumstances of the courses they were taking or the approach they were following would transform them.

Those who had made the fundamental choice to have the life they wanted, on the other hand, were not at all passive about their success. They actively sought out and put into practice whatever might be useful to them.

In the movie *Rocky*, the dramatic turning point occurred when Rocky made a fundamental choice to be the best he could be in his life, to commit himself to himself.

Even though he had been a club boxer for years, he had never fully involved himself in his sport. In the movie, one symbol of this was his nose. In all his years of boxing, he proudly boasted that his nose had never been broken.

Through a strange set of circumstances, Rocky became the challenger in a world title fight. While training for the fight, his trainer confronted Rocky about his lack of commitment, and demanded of Rocky that he fully commit himself to do the best he possibly could, whether he won or lost. Rocky made that fundamental choice. From that moment on he fully applied himself to his training, including inventing new ways of developing his boxing abilities.

Most people assumed Rocky would last at most one or two rounds with the champion. In fact, he lasted the entire fight and tied the champion in points, according to the scoring judges. In one of the early rounds of the fight, Rocky broke his nose—a symbol of his total commitment and involvement in what he was doing.

After the fight, in spite of the cuts, bruises, and exhaustion he had endured, he said he had never felt better in his whole life. The experience Rocky had was that his whole life had changed from the moment he had made that fundamental choice.

In film sequels to Rocky, fundamental choice played a central role in each drama. Once a choice is made, you, like Rocky, may need to re-make it from time to time.

As time and circumstances change, you may lose touch with what you most deeply care about. But since the truth is that you do deeply care about these choices, you are easily able to re-make them.

IMPORTANT FUNDAMENTAL CHOICES

When a person makes a choice to create something in particular out of endless possibilities, Martin Buber describes the force involved as "direction." In his book, *Daniel: Conversations about Realizations*, Buber explains what "direction" means to him.

> Direction is that primal tension of the human soul which moves it at times out of the infinity of the possible to choose this and nothing else, and to realize it through action.

In his concern for the future of civilization, Buber calls for us to be conscious of our fundamental choices. In Buber's terminology, to make fundamental choices would be "to act with direction."

The choices that for most people are fundamental are the choices to be free, to be healthy, and to be true to oneself.

Freedom finds both inner and outer expression. Outer freedom includes to the ability to choose and create the circumstances of your life. Inner freedom, or spiritual freedom, includes the experience of limitlessness.

Health refers to physical, mental, emotional, and spiritual well-being, separately and collectively.

Being true to yourself means living in accordance with your essential nature and morality, and fulfilling the individual and unique purpose of your life.

As I mentioned before, a fundamental choice has to do with your life orientation or state of being. Thus, *the fundamental choice in making the shift to the orientation of the creative is the fundamental choice to be the predominant creative force in your life.* This is a key choice in living up to your fullest potential. Without it, you experience more struggle and insecurity, because you still see the circumstances in your life as the dominant forces, and yourself as subject to them.

SOME QUALITIES OF A FUNDAMENTAL CHOICE

Fundamental choices are not subject to changes in internal or external circumstances. If you make the fundamental choice to be true to yourself, then you will act in ways that are true to yourself whether you feel inspired or depressed, whether you feel fulfilled or frustrated, whether you are at home, at work, with your friends or with your enemies.

If, on the other hand, a man one day decides it is all right not to be true to himself because it is inconvenient or might make him feel uncomfortable in a particular situation, he has probably never made the fundamental choice to be true to himself to begin with. His commitment to himself is based on the conditions or the circumstances in which he happens to find himself at any particular time. When a fundamental choice is made, convenience and comfort are not ever at issue, for action is always taken based on what is consistent with the fundamental choice.

In the championship fight, Rocky demonstrated tremendous courage and character. A number of times Rocky's trainer wanted to throw in the towel to end the fight, but Rocky was determined to see it through. He was experiencing life differently since he had made the choice to be the best that he could be.

Once the fundamental choice is made, an entirely new basis for dealing with reality becomes available. The meaning of circumstances often shifts because of a fundamental choice. You begin looking to see how circumstances, no matter what they may be, can work toward the fulfillment of your fundamental choice.

If your fundamental choice is to be true to yourself, you look at the circumstances and use that information to make any adjustments of the circumstances that you need to make in order to be true to yourself.

David worked as a stockbroker for a large investment firm. He often complained about the difficult circumstances of his job and of his company. Once he had made the fundamental choice to be true to himself however, he was able to change his relationship to the circumstances at work, from acting as if he were a victim of them to using them as necessary feedback.

One of his most common complaints had been about his boss, whom he often criticized as being unhelpful to him. After David had made his fundamental choice, he committed himself to supporting his boss as best he could. As a result, David's entire experience at work changed. He personally became a much more effective stock-broker for his clients, and he went from being unsatisfied with his job to being deeply satisfied. Instead of looking to his work to satisfy him, he brought his own satisfaction to his work.

In the reactive-responsive orientation, people look to the circumstances to provide them with satisfaction. They are inevitably disappointed, because circumstances themselves do not provide satisfaction.

In the orientation of the creative, it is not circumstances which bring you satisfaction. You create your own satisfaction, independent of the circumstances. Then you bring satisfaction to those circumstances in which you are involved.

You need never look to the various projects in which you are involved to bring you satisfaction. Therefore, you never have to guess or speculate which projects will bring you satisfaction. You need only consider whether or not you care enough about those projects to be involved with them, knowing that whatever you do, you will bring to it your own level of satisfaction. When you choose to be involved with a project, there is no ulterior motive–you are not looking to see what you can get out of it. There is only your enthusiasm and commitment–to see the results of the project fulfilled.

Once you have made any fundamental choice, say, to be true to yourself, a new structure is created, and the path of least resistance in that structure leads toward the fulfillment of your fundamental choice. In this new structure, you might find yourself suddenly easily able to give up unwanted compromises. You might suddenly stop old habits such as gossiping, being petty, complaining, blaming others, or looking for sympathy. These old habits would cease based on the strength and power of your commitment to the fundamental choice, and not because you tried to manipulate yourself into giving them up.

One of the approaches in which I train psychotherapists is in the use of choice. I encourage them to have their clients first know what they want out of therapy (primary choice). I also recommend they explain to their clients the dynamics of secondary choices. A major step is to have the therapists then encourage their clients to make the fundamental choices to be whole, healthy, free, and true to themselves. For most, these fundamental choices, when made, create a new orientation toward life. Until such an orientation is chosen, little effective or lasting therapeutic work can be done.

PRIMARY CHOICE AND FUNDAMENTAL CHOICE

A primary choice is about concrete results, while a fundamental choice is about life-orientation or a state of being.

I can make a primary choice to be a symphony musician and make all the secondary choices to successfully achieve my primary choice, without making a fundamental choice to live up to my highest potential.

Or I can successfully make primary choices to have a well painted house, an organized closet, or an interesting career, without making the fundamental choice to be the predominant creative force in my life.

There are many people who have chosen the religious path (primary choice), without making the fundamental choice to live in accordance with the highest spiritual truths.

There are many people who have chosen to be married (primary choice), without making the fundamental choice to live from within a committed relationship.

FUNDAMENTAL CHOICE AND THE REACTIVE-RESPONSIVE ORIENTATION

In the reactive-responsive orientation, one's state of being may be described as primarily reactive or primarily responsive. Most people who are primarily oriented toward being subject to internal or external circumstantial stimuli have probably never made a fundamental choice about their own lives.

It is important to note that a fundamental life choice does not have to be formally made. Some people are true to themselves even though they never made a formal choice to be so. But by the way they live their lives they have made, in essence, a *de facto* fundamental choice to be true to themselves. By formalizing that choice, however, they can begin to live even more easily from within the power of that choice.

A fundamental choice can provide the crucial difference in successfully making the shift from the reactive-responsive orientation to the orientation of the creative. Without making the fundamental choice to be the predominant creative force in your life, no matter what you do to attempt to benefit yourself or enhance your life you will, structurally, merely be finding more sophisticated ways of responding to circumstantial stimuli. This will, in turn, reinforce your reactive-responsive orientation. No primary choice will substitute for this fundamental choice. Making primary choices, no matter what the primary choices are and no matter how many you make, can never shift you out of the reactive-responsive orientation. Furthermore, the things you do within the reactive-responsive orientation to attempt to better yourself can give you the impression of change and movement, but it is not likely that any significant change will take place. Even if your attempts seem to work temporarily, they do not fulfill your true desires.

On the other hand, once you make the fundamental choice to be the predominant creative force in your life, any approach you choose to take for your own growth and development can work, and you will be especially attracted to those approaches which will work particularly well for you.

This one fundamental choice–to be the predominant creative force in your life–is the foundation for the entire orientation of the creative. Once you have made this choice, the meaning of current reality changes for you, from circumstances externally imposed to relevant and necessary feedback in the creative process. The meaning of desire changes for you, from idle wishes and hopes to true vision of that which is highest in human aspiration and vision. The meaning of human endeavor changes from actions taken in an attempt to regain emotional stability to actions taken to bring into the world the full realization of the vision you hold.

Moreover, the entire quality of your life changes dramatically, from the tragedy, drudgery, pain, tolerance, struggle, sameness and boredom so often characteristic of life in the reactive-responsive orientation to the enjoyment and adventure characteristic of life in the orientation of the creative. In this orientation, every moment holds the potential for true expression of the human spirit, where anything good and wonderful may happen.

EMOTIONS, ATTITUDES OR BEHAVIOR

In comparing the quality of life in the two orientations, I am not talking merely of emotional responses but of states of being. To use a medical analogy, for those in the reactive-responsive orientation, it is as if their quality of life is described by a body living in a state anywhere from continuous low grade infection to terminal illness, while in the orientation of the creative it is as if the body enjoys robust health.

The shift from the reactive-responsive orientation to the creative path is not an emotional change nor is it a change in attitudes. It is a change in fundamental orientation; it is a change in the structure of your life. In fact, many of your attitudes may remain unchanged when you make a shift of orientation. You may still dislike certain people, you may still get angry at pettiness in the office, you may still get discouraged at your financial situation. You may still hold the same political or religious beliefs. You may still prefer to live in certain cities and areas of the country. You may still be the negative, critical, judgmental, cranky person you have always been. A fundamental shift in orientation is not primarily about a change in attitudes, style or manner of living.

However, the *meaning* of these characteristics changes considerably when you make a shift to the creative orientation.

As a character, Rocky had always been compassionate, sincere, and caring, and yet his life suffered from uninvolvement. Once he had made his fundamental choice to be the best he could be, no matter what, those special qualities he possessed came into focus and he was more able to express them fully.

When you make a fundamental choice you bring into play the qualities of your character, so that they can be more fully expressed in your life. Each of them becomes an element in your current reality and thus part of your creative process.

Furthermore, this shift in orientation is not primarily about behavior, but about the underlying creative structure now in play. Behavior will, of course, change. But it will change, as it changed for Rocky and for David the stockbroker, as a natural outcome of a change in structure, for the path of least resistance in the creative orientation leads toward behavior which is consistent with creating what you want to create.

When you attempt to change behavior artificially–say, by using manipulation or force–with no real change in the underlying structure which gives rise to that behavior, the path of least resistance leads back to the original behavior.

It is even possible to maintain a synthetic or artificial change in behavior for many years. But without a real change in underlying structure, maintaining the new behavior consumes enormous amounts of energy, since you are constantly moving against the path of least resistance.

So what can this change be that I am describing, if it is not a change in behavior, emotions, attitudes, or style of living?

It is a change in the very structure of your being, which determines your ability to manifest on the planet that which is highest in you. This change is initiated by making the fundamental choice to be the predominant creative force in your life.

HOW TO MAKE THIS FUNDAMENTAL CHOICE

The way to make a fundamental choice is essentially the same as the way to make a primary choice.

First of all, you must want whatever it is you are choosing. This step is essential. If you do not really want to be the predominant creative force in your life, you cannot make that fundamental choice.

If this want is not clearly desired for its own sake, the choice you make does not qualify as a fundamental choice. You may choose to be free, for example, only because you feel unfree. In this, you are choosing out of reaction to being unfree. You are not making the fundamental choice to be free, because you are not yet in touch with wanting to be free, but only with not wanting to be unfree. Under these circumstances, if you then "choose to be free," it would be meaningless as a fundamental choice, for structurally it has no chance of having any significant impact on your freedom.

To truly make the fundamental choice to be free, first you must recognize what freedom really is and be aware that freedom is what you want. "If you could have it, would you take it?" If the answer is yes, then freedom is what you want. In making this fundamental choice, if you know that you want freedom, independent of past, present, or future circumstances, you can easily and clearly make the fundamental choice to be free.

The fundamental choice to be free is one of the choices integral to a complete shift from the reactive-responsive orientation to the orientation of the creative. Here are the steps to take to make the full and complete shift.

Step 1 is to know what you want. To do this, consider whether you want each of the following items. Do not assume that you automatically want them. In fact, make no assumptions. Start without any preconceived notions. My suggestion is that you spend at least two minutes, but no more than five, considering each item:

   Item 1. Being the predominant creative force in your life
   Item 2. Being true to yourself
   Item 3. Health (physical, emotional, mental, spiritual)
   Item 4. Freedom.

Step 2 is to choose what you want.

If you want freedom, health, being true to yourself, and being the predominant creative force in your life, then inwardly formally choose each of them in turn. Say to yourself:

   I choose to be the predominant creative force in my life
   I choose to be true to myself
   I choose to be healthy
   I choose to be free.

THE EFFECTS OF FUNDAMENTAL CHOICES

If you have made these choices, over time you may begin to observe natural changes and shifts in the way you live your life. You may notice changes in how free you are, how healthy you are, how true you are to yourself, and how fully and effectively you create the results you want. These changes develop from within the new orientation and its structure. Your natural tendency will be to gravitate toward reorganizing your life in ways that are consistent with these four fundamental choices. Circumstances may change slowly or quickly. But once you have made these choices, time is on your side, for the structural tendencies of your life are now designed to fulfill those choices.

Your natural temptation at this point would probably be to ask for an example of how this shift might look in a person's life. But in the creative orientation, we cannot predict what the shift will look like, for it will be unique in each case. In fact, it is probably more useful not to have a model or picture of how it might look, because then your temptation would be to try matching your reality to the picture in the example.

Though Beethoven and Mozart were both great composers, Beethoven's long, tedious creative process was very different from Mozart's quick, brilliant creative process. Your way of creating the life you want will unfold differently from anyone else's.

If you have read this far without making the four fundamental choices, I recommend that you go back and consider those four items. And if you want them, choose them.

I could describe the taste of vanilla ice cream to you, but until you have tasted vanilla ice cream for yourself, you would not know what I was describing. Actually making those four fundamental choices is quite different from just reading about them. The best way to experience the power of fundamental choices is by making them.

CHAPTER 14

ASSIMILATION

A NATURAL AND NORMAL STAGE

Assimilation is one of the most natural and normal stages of growth and development.

We are all very familiar with assimilation, for we experience it as children when learning to walk (as we assimilate and incorporate the skills of balance and movement), when learning to talk (as we assimilate and incorporate the vocabulary and syntax of our native language), when learning to write (as we assimilate the shapes of letters and words and the muscle movements required to make them with a pencil or pen), and when learning to ride a bicycle (as we assimilate the skill of keeping ourselves balanced while we pedal the bicycle forward).

We continue using assimilation throughout our adult lives. When we learn to drive a car, we assimilate and coordinate all the movements of feet and hands required to maneuver the car smoothly and safely.

Assimilation is an important stage of growth and development because it is the period during which we incorporate skills in such a way that they become a natural part of ourselves. Yet assimilation remains poorly understood.

THE BEGINNINGS OF ASSIMILATION

One reason this stage is so misunderstood is that during it, progress in growth and development remains invisible for a time.

Sometimes even for long periods it looks as if nothing of significance is happening or being learned. A common experience during the early steps of assimilation is that no change whatever is taking place.

Since the first excitement of the germinational stage is over, and since the new development occurring is still at its least obvious point in the growth cycle, this is often the moment when people give up the pursuit of their desired result.

This is the point when music students give up trying to learn to play their musical instruments. This is the time when most people who enter exercise or fitness programs give up. This is the time when many adults who want to learn a foreign language lose interest or become "too busy to continue."

The emotional experiences common to this crucial stage in the creative cycle are discomfort, frustration, and disappointment because nothing seems to be happening and no progress seems to be being made. The beginnings of the assimilation stage can be uncomfortable.

In the reactive-responsive orientation, the path of least resistance at this stage leads you to give up. Giving up is an attempt to avoid emotional frustration and disappointment.

In the orientation of the creative, the crucial moment at the beginning of the assimilation stage where nothing seems to be happening is not a threat, for two major reasons.

The first reason is this: it is understood by people in the creative orientation that there will be periods of time in the creative process during which, superficially, nothing seems to be happening. They understand further that these periods do not inhibit the development of the result being created but, in fact, enhance it. This understanding comes from experience. People know that learning to ride a bicycle includes a period of time—maybe a day, maybe a week—during which the learners frequently lose their balance and fall off the bicycle. Many people find that during their first attempts at wind surfing they are more often in the water than on the surfboard.

This period of assimilation naturally includes much trial, error, and experimentation. But the outcomes of such experiments teach you what you need to learn in order to have the result you want. Losing your balance and falling off the bicycle or wind surfboard is seen not as failure, but as a moment of learning.

You absorb such learning as part of your knowledge and ability.

Assimilation is a step beyond mere learning, for in assimilation you incorporate the learning as your own. Moreover, the very habit of learning in this way becomes part of your general knowledge and ability. In other words, you not only learn a specific skill, but you also learn that you can learn and you learn that you can assimilate whatever you need to know in any creative process.

There is a second reason the early moments of assimilation are not seen as a threat in the orientation of the creative. Even if it seems as though nothing has changed or no real progress has been made toward achieving the desired result, that very observation becomes part of the description of current reality. As such, it reinforces structural tension by highlighting the discrepancy between what you now have and the result you want.

DEEPENING ASSIMILATION

Assimilation deepens as you move toward the realization of your vision.

When I first attended the Boston Conservatory of Music, the clarinetist Attilio Poto was one of my teachers. The first lesson he assigned me was a bit more difficult than I was technically ready for. After a week of diligent practice I still couldn't play it very well. When I went for my second lesson, I expected that Mr. Poto would have me spend at least another week practicing the same exercise. Instead, he assigned the next exercise in the book, which was even more difficult than the one with which I had struggled for the past week.

I spent the week attempting to play the new exercise, and when the time came for my lesson I could not play it very well. I suggested to Mr. Poto that it was time to perfect my technique by focusing on that exercise for another week. Mr. Poto only smiled as he turned the page to the next, and more difficult, exercise in the book.

For three more weeks, I was assigned progressively more difficult exercises to play, each of which I was unable to play well after a week of practice.

At the sixth lesson, Mr. Poto turned back to the very first exercise he had assigned me—my exercise for the first week—and asked me to play it. Although I had not even looked at that exercise for the past five weeks, I was able to play it well. He then turned to the second week's exercise and, again, I was able to play it well.

Had I spent six weeks attempting to perfect those first two exercises, I would not have been able to play them as well as I did that day.

Mr. Poto knew something about assimilation that I was only beginning to learn: *one way to assimilate your present step is by moving on to your next step,* even if you feel inadequately prepared for that next step. When you move to your next step, you are somehow able to incorporate more than you now know about your present step.

ASSIMILATION AS AN INNER PROCESS

Assimilation is an inner process. And it is important to recognize that growth during this stage takes place within. In the early stages of pregnancy the fetus being developed is not immediately obvious to anyone, but assimilation is taking place within the mother.

In the creative process, once you have activated the seeds of your creation by conceiving and choosing the results you want, the next stage of growth develops within you. As a newly planted seed begins to establish itself in the soil first by sending out roots, so the vision you have germinated is also taking root within your structural makeup.

Once the plant's basic root system is established, the path of least resistance in that structure is for the plant to sprout through the ground and begin to become visible.

So with you in the orientation of the creative, the path of least resistance leads that which you have germinated to begin to sprout and finally to become visible.

ASSIMILATION AS ORGANIC

Assimilation is a natural and organic form of development. In 1970–71, I spent much reflective time in the woods making observations about changes and cycles in nature. As a composer, I was interested in isolating principles of structure that I could use in my music. During that year, I began to have a deeper appreciation for the principle that new forms emerge from the disintegration of old forms–moss growing upon dead tree trunks, seedlings sprouting through dead leaves. These changes of growth and decay had a rightness to them, a rightness which permeated the entire woods as an organic system.

In the creative process a similar kind of rightness exists, particularly in the assimilation stage of the creative cycle. As an organic process, assimilation generates actions, some of which naturally build new and useful structures and some of which naturally discard outmoded and less useful structures.

Roger was a golfer who had played in the same style for the past twelve years. His usual score was in the low 90's. He decided to improve his game significantly. The result he wanted was a score in the low 70's. Over a period of several weeks, playing once or twice a week, he found himself during his drives beginning to move his body in ways which were atypical for him. He began to grip his clubs differently, his stance subtly changed, and his swing changed noticeably. These changes marked a shift from his old form, which was less useful and outmoded, to a new form which gave his playing more power and accuracy. He was able to improve his score to the mid 70's. Roger's change of golf style was a natural outcome of assimilation, as he embodied being the golfer he wanted to be.

EMBODIMENT: THE KEY TO ASSIMILATION

The principle that *what you embody tends to be created* provides the key to assimilation.

That which you embody is distinct from behavior. To embody love is not the same as behaving in a loving style. To embody peace is not the same as acting serenely.

What is truly going on within you is what you embody. Those who "fight for peace" do not embody peace, but rather embody fighting. On the other hand, Martin Luther King, Jr., did embody the values he championed. He embodied freedom, peace, and justice, which is one major reason his vision had such great impact on the history of the United States.

Why is embodiment the key to assimilation? When you embody something, especially if it is something you want to see created, you hold it in yourself and it eventually becomes a part of you.

What you embody speaks louder than your behavior, to the same degree that your actions speak louder than your words.

You do not become a good golfer until you embody being a good golfer. You do not become a good musician until you embody being a good musician. The same goes for being a good lawyer, machinist, typist, or any other type of professional.

You can, however, make a fundamental choice to be a master typist before you can actually type well. Such a fundamental choice will enable you to learn to master typing more quickly, because embodiment produces momentum.

And you assimilate what you embody. As you internalize what you embody inner development occurs that is consistent with what you embody. All aspects of your consciousness realign themselves in accordance with what you embody. When this restructuring occurs, as it did in Martin Luther King, Jr., the path of least resistance changes, and energy is able to flow directly through the system, aligning external reality with internal reality.

In King's early life he experienced hatred for those who subjected black people to the injustice of racial prejudice. In his personal development he came to embody peace and unconditional love, which changed his relationship with the situations and the people he was addressing. His nonviolent approach was only made possible by the inner strength and power resulting from the commitment to freedom and justice he embodied.

Assimilation, like embodiment, has two phases—an internalizing phase and an externalizing phase. The growth begins internally and expands to the external. A human fetus grows within a pregnant woman, at first virtually invisible and then expanding until the child is ready to be born. What you create grows within you and eventually expresses itself outwardly as you give birth to that which you are creating.

During the assimilation process, inner and outer resources and actions are mobilized. This energy builds on itself, so that the path of least resistance leads from internal to external expression.

When you truly learn a new language, you assimilate it. At first, the language is foreign to you. Little by little you take it in as you practice it. The more you embrace it, the more it becomes a part of you. This is the internalizing phase of assimilation. As you internalize the new language you become more fluent. You are able to construct sentences and learn vocabulary and syntax which are more and more conceptually sophisticated. The language becomes fully internalized, so that you can think in that language, imagine in that language, and even dream in that language.

The externalizing phase of assimilation occurs when you begin to speak and communicate with others spontaneously in that language. You retain new vocabulary easily, you use it naturally. In fact, you are able to speak, write and create things you were never taught. When you are around people who speak that language, the path of least resistance leads you to speak it too.

USING ASSIMILATION IN YOUR LIFE

What you assimilate internally tends to be manifested externally. Internal changes often tend to be manifested outwardly.

You will not be able to create change in all your external circumstances, but you can certainly create change in your internal realm. You may not have access directly to change the world, but you have complete access to changing yourself. You do not need anyone's permission or agreement. You do not have to wait for outside resources to show up. In the orientation of the creative, you begin any act of creation by having everything you need.

Since internal changes have impact and influence on external circumstances, ultimately there is nothing beyond your reach. Such is the power of the creative process when it is mastered. In order to master the creative process, you need to master the stage of assimilation, and then to build momentum.

CHAPTER 15

MOMENTUM

HOW ASSIMILATION BUILDS MOMENTUM

Assimilation is a graduated process. It occurs in steps. These steps build upon one another. As they build organically, the process generates energy. This energy builds on itself, and the process gains momentum.

The more you assimilate the early steps of a growth or learning process–as in learning mathematics, cooking, sewing, accounting, computer science, or a foreign language–the more able you are to assimilate the next steps. And once those steps are assimilated, momentum builds and you are able to assimilate steps that are even more advanced. In fact, assimilation becomes easier and easier.

It is easier to learn a new foreign language if you already speak a foreign language than if you don't. By learning a foreign language, not only do you assimilate that language, but you also assimilate your ability to learn other languages. If you speak two foreign languages, it is even easier to learn a third.

There is often a kind of exponential growth quality about assimilation: assimilating one thing makes it easier to assimilate more and more other things. In fact, in the orientation of the creative, once you have assimilated your own creative process, your life mastery in general increases, so that you are enabled more naturally and easily to create those things that most matter to you.

The assimilation process is one which builds. This building process takes place over a period of time. Therefore, in assimilation change is not instantaneous but rather developmental. In Japan, it takes seven years to master the art of sushi-making. It often takes over twenty years to master the cello. It usually takes ten years or more to become a master cabinetmaker. Making fine cabinets, playing the cello, or mastering the art of sushi-making cannot be done overnight.

Mastering your life-building process in the orientation of the creative is not an instantaneous transformation either, because one inextricable part of the creative process is assimilation, which can occur only over a period of time.

And yet, mastering your life-building process can take less time than learning to master making sushi–for most people, a period of two or three years is all they need.

This would be two or three years well spent. I can think of nothing else that could have such total positive impact on all of your life–and for the rest of your life.

The reason mastering your life-building process is not the most difficult activity you could undertake is that it is very natural to human life.

ASSIMILATION AS GENERATIVE

Not only is assimilation an organic process itself, but it tends to generate other organic processes, as it did with the different elements of Roger's golf game. This means that the steps by which you move from where you are in your life to where you want to be cannot be put into a formula. The steps of that process develop organically, and what you are creating is unique, at least to your life. You may find yourself taking actions you have never taken before, thinking thoughts you have never thought before, being moved and inspired in ways you have never experienced before.

If you try synthetically to control the process by which you will move from where you are to where you want to be, as is often attempted in the reactive-responsive orientation, you will block true assimilation. Trying to control the process limits the possibilities of what can happen in your life. Furthermore, in this orientation, actions that you take do not generate further actions. Each step you take toward your goal must be taken by itself, without the benefits of the momentum which come from assimilation. Each new step remains at the same level of difficulty as previous steps. And many of the steps which would be crucial to creating the result you want will not even occur to you.

Because assimilation is an essential stage in the creative process, when you try to act without it, it is as if you are pitted against the universe and you must strive to overcome the natural forces.

With assimilation, however, it is as if the universe is cooperating with you as you work aligned with the natural forces. When you utilize assimilation, each step you take teaches you about the next steps. The energy you apply toward what you are creating regenerates and builds. Needed resources somehow begin to gather themselves. The organic process of assimilation may include unusual "coincidences" which lead directly to where you want to be. In the structure of assimilation, the path of least resistance leads toward building momentum.

MOMENTUM

For people in the reactive-responsive orientation, momentum is one of the most difficult and elusive properties of growth and development to understand and use. When you are in that orientation you do not build momentum toward achieving the results you want. You experience only shifts of conflict which create momentary bursts of energy, as you take action designed to avoid or reduce the discomfort associated with the conflict.

The energy that moves through the conflictual structure is certainly not momentum, because there is no growth-in-energy factor. Furthermore, each step taken remains a single isolated action–like a reflex knee-jerk reaction–unrelated to any other actions and designed only to resolve the specific conflict at hand. For every conflict there is a reaction. In the reactive-responsive orientation, each action-reaction situation is an isolated event, leading nowhere in particular.

In the orientation of the creative you are naturally and easily able to build momentum. Every action you take, whether it is directly successful or not, adds additional energy to your path. Because of this, everything you do works toward creating eventual success, including those things which are not immediately successful. Over a period of time, creating the results you want gets easier and easier.

A river bed is structured in such a way that the water flows along a path of least resistance. As more water is added, the flow gains momentum, and the general force of all the water moving through that structure increases.

LEARNING TO BUILD MOMENTUM

All successful entrepreneurs have learned to build momentum. A woman I know wanted to create her own real estate business. In the beginning of her new venture she worked alone, ten to twelve hours each day. After four years she had reached a point where she had twenty employees, and her business was viable and successful. She then began a second business, a landscaping and lawn care service. This time, as she built on her experience, skills, and business contacts from real estate, the new business became viable and successful in two years. As an entrepreneur, she was then in an even stronger position to create a third and fourth business–a referral service for housekeepers and cooks, and one for handymen–based on the momentum she had built up.

As she built momentum, she also expanded her capacity to produce successful businesses. Four or five years after her first success she had much more capacity for success, including financial resources, human resources, know-how, and contact with a growing number of people who could help her. Through momentum, she developed her capacity to attract to herself the kinds of people who could manage her organizations. She actually has more free time now than she had five years ago, even though she now owns four companies.

When you assimilate the actions that you take, you build energy toward new actions. What the entrepreneur was able to do was to let each action she took become a part of her. With all of these steps incorporated as part of her development, every step she took was both a step toward her goal and, even more importantly, a step in learning to use such movement to build momentum toward attaining any future goals.

Momentum is more than self-consciously learning from your actions, whether they happen to be successes or mistakes. For the successful businesswoman, momentum meant building her entrepreneurial muscles. She was able to incorporate into herself the additive power provided by each business step she took, in the same way that body builders incorporate within their muscles the increased strength and endurance that comes from regular exercise.

HOW TO USE MOMENTUM

What is the difference between the way this entrepreneur achieved results and the way most people go after their goals?

First of all, she was building momentum rather than problem-solving. Each step of the way she was able to use whatever happened as a learning experience which taught her how to build momentum more effectively.

Second, she looked for new ways to build momentum. She experimented and sought out challenges. At first she tried selling properties that were beyond her present ability. She sought, for example, to broker a large commercial tract. She learned from her lack of success that she was reaching too far. Because the reaching out was too complex for her at that point, she could not assimilate it or use it to build momentum. She shifted her attention to a simpler approach, selling private homes, and chose projects that were more easily accomplished. Then she began looking for, and being attracted to, projects that were within her range yet still offered her a challenge. Challenge helped build momentum. As time went on, she kept expanding.

Third, she learned that experience helps build momentum. Every project she undertook seemed to teach her many lessons about being an entrepreneur. Even when projects were not successful, she learned new techniques. She learned to coordinate administration, finances, and decisions. During her early years she kept her risks low so that she would not go out of business while she was learning what she needed to learn. Each decision she made taught her how to make decisions; the ones that worked taught her about the qualities of successful decisions, the ones that did not work taught her about the qualities of ineffective decisions. All the time, she was gaining perspective about her entire area of business.

As she incorporated the learning into herself, she could step back and see the broader sweep of her business with greater and greater perspective. From this perspective, she was able to anticipate developments in her field and make decisions based on her foresight. More and more, the path of least resistance led her toward increasing success, and each success supported and built momentum toward still greater success.

THE PLACE OF STANDARD FORMULAS

Because she assimilated the actions she took, she became the expert on her individual creative process. While conventional wisdom was also available for her use, she was never confined or limited to it. What she was doing, in fact, was inventing her own steps along the way and developing her own unique method of creating what she wanted. If she had relied only on standard formulas prescribing how to run a successful business, she never would have been able to build the momentum she did or to assimilate the steps she took. She was able to build momentum and assimilate the steps only because she made them her own. There was no business school in the country that could have taught her all she needed to know, for what she needed to know was specifically tailored to her own unique situation.

In the reactive-responsive orientation, there is always the temptation to rely on formulas which prescribe how to respond in various situations. When you attempt to learn to create by formula, no fundamental change occurs in the underlying structure, and the path of least resistance continues to lead exactly where it has always led.

"The human tendency toward the fossilizing of form is shocking, even tragic," wrote painter Wassily Kandinsky in a letter to composer Arnold Schoenberg. "Yesterday the man who exhibited a new form was condemned. Today the same form has become immovable law for all time. This is tragic because it shows over and over again that human beings depend mostly on externals."

Pioneers like Kandinsky and Schoenberg understood that they needed to invent new forms of expression along the way. They did this not for the sake of the forms themselves or to create an artistic school or movement, but to express their artistic visions.

As Schoenberg put it in a letter to Kandinsky, "I have long felt that our period—which is, after all, a great one—will bring forth not one, but many possibilities."

Schoenberg was embarrassed by those who called themselves "atonalists" and claimed to be his followers. "Damn it all," he told Kandinsky, "I did my composing without any isms in mind. What has it got to do with me? Personally, I haven't much taste for all these movements, but at least I don't have to worry that they'll imitate me for long. Nothing comes to a standstill sooner than movements that are brought about by so many people."

In the orientation of the creative you are on your own. Even if you find a book or a course which provides you with helpful information, you still need to assimilate this information by making it your own and applying it to your particular situation to create momentum. In the creative orientation, when you are able to assimilate the steps along the way, as the entrepreneur did, the underlying structure reorganizes itself, so that the path of least resistance leads directly toward what you want to create. And the increasing momentum helps move you along that path more and more effectively.

ASSIMILATING STRUCTURAL TENSION

When you first begin to learn any skill, there is usually a large component of conscious awareness involved in the process. When you begin learning to drive you need to think consciously what pedal your foot is touching and how much pressure to apply. You must consciously think about how to turn the steering wheel, when to shift, how to use the rearview mirror, how to gauge distance, how to back up, how to parallel park, and so on.

Once you assimilate these abilities, you no longer need to consider consciously how much pressure you need to apply to the brake pedal in order to stop the car smoothly and safely. When you want to stop or slow down you automatically carry out the necessary movements.

When you first begin to use structural tension in creating a specific result, you must consciously hold in mind both your vision (the result you want to create) and current reality (your present circumstances). As you consciously practice simultaneously focusing on your vision and observing current reality, you begin to be able to assimilate this action, and eventually it becomes an automatic habit. You also naturally incorporate structual tension itself as a major force in your underlying structural makeup.

Many years ago I moved to Los Angeles. When I first arrived, I was surprised to hear the local people tell me that they had snow. Having never heard of snow in Los Angeles before, I asked, "When do you have snow?"

"When we drive to the mountains two hours away," they answered.

Because I grew up in New England, my concept of having snow was quite different. For me, snow wasn't something you went to visit. Snow visited *you*. You lived with it.

When you first begin to work with structural tension, you will have a tendency only to "visit" it. It will not be included in your normal way of life. But as you work with structural tension more and more, it will become assimilated into your life. Rather than visit it, you will find that it becomes part of your reality. When that happens, you will automatically be aware at any moment of what you want to create and what truly matters to you and you will observe the prevailing circumstances of your current reality. When that happens, you will also automatically begin to be able to create momentum.

Assimilation itself will also become natural and automatic to you. As you begin to achieve the results you want, new or more far reaching results become easier, because you have assimilated structural tension and the orientation of the creative. Through your assimilation of structural tension, you begin to master your own creative process. And creating with momentum becomes the dominant orientation of your life.

TIME DELAY

When you first begin to make changes in your life, there is often a delay between the time you initiate the change and the time you begin to see the results of the change.

Often a result does not immediately follow the action you took to bring about the result. Therefore it is possible to initiate effective changes but not know, for a period of time, that they are effective.

If you go on a diet, you expect to lose weight. But if just before going on the diet you ate a very big meal, you might actually gain weight on the first day of your diet.

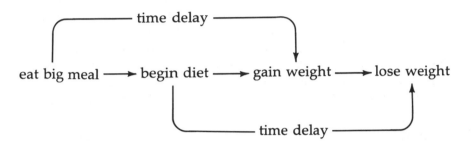

At this point, an immediate temptation would be to conclude that dieting causes weight gain or that this diet does not work for you. What is going on, however, is that the result of the diet has not yet had a chance to appear. There is a time delay between action and result.

The way you define results is a crucial part of the creative process. If you had defined gaining weight, which is the result of eating a big meal, as if it had been the result of beginning your diet, you would probably have stopped your diet.

Because of time delay people often give up doing actions which are in fact effective, but the result of which has not yet had a chance to appear. The meaning you give to the actions you take can contribute either to building or to reducing momentum.

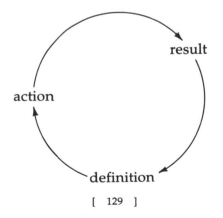

Action produces a result; a result gives rise to a definition or meaning. *How you define the relation between the action and the result affects future action.* It also affects momentum.

E. L. Doctorow, author of the famous novel *Ragtime*, sent his first novel *The Book of Daniel* to publisher after publisher. For years, he received rejection slips in the mail. The action he took, sending the manuscript, was followed by the result of the manuscript not being accepted. Had he defined this result to mean "my novel is not worthy of publication," that definition would have affected his future actions; he would have lost momentum and would not have sent the manuscript to other publishers.

What he actually did was define the meaning of the result (each rejection slip) as "that was not the right publisher for my book." This definition affected his future actions, for he kept his momentum going and continued to send the manuscript to other publishers until he found the right one, the publisher who was able to recognize the value of his novel.

In the creative orientation, when you move toward the full accomplishment of the result you choose there may be delays along the way. For some people, these cause great frustration and trepidation. But as you continue to move forward toward your result, these moments often become strategic, for they present important opportunities to catalyze the creative process.

CHAPTER 16

STRATEGIC MOMENTS

APPARENT LACK OF PROGRESS

In the creative process, there are certain strategic moments in which it seems as if you are either standing still or even going backwards. These moments of apparent lack of progress are strategic because the actions you take at such moments will determine to a large degree whether or not you are ultimately successful.

A novice hiker backpacking on the Appalachian trail was standing on top of one mountain. The peak of a neighboring mountain seemed only half a mile away. He set out in the direction of the second mountain, only to find himself in a valley much deeper than he had expected. He had already walked at least two miles. From his vantage point in the valley it appeared that he was now farther away from the second mountaintop than when he had first seen it.

Often you assume you are closer to your desired result than you actually are. When the novice backpacker was in the valley, it seemed to him that he was further from his destination than he had been when he started, but actually he was closer. He had not moved away from the second mountaintop, losing ground, but was actually moving toward it. In the same way, there are moments in the creative process when it seems that you are farther away from your result than when you began, but in fact you are closer to it.

The backpacker was at a strategic moment in his quest. He could have made either of two assumptions. He could have assumed that the path which seemed to lead toward the mountain was actually leading him away from the mountain. Or he could have assumed that the second peak was farther away than he first thought. Of course, he realized that the second assumption was true, and the first one false. However, the situation in the creative process is not always as clear as it was for the backpacker.

When you attempt to move in the direction of results you want, there are times when you discover that the route to those results is more involved or longer than you originally thought. The difference between our mountain example and the creative process is that the backpacker knew that if he continued walking, he would eventually reach the second mountaintop. At such a strategic moment in the creative process, it is not always clear that you will reach the result you have in mind.

One of the more difficult lessons to learn is to *recognize current reality as it now is*, which often is different from what you think it is supposed to be or how you want it to be.

RESENTING CURRENT REALITY

If you find yourself continually resenting the fact that your present circumstances are not what you expected, you hinder your ability to use the power of current reality fully in creating structural tension.

If you are on a white water rafting trip, you need to be able to recognize current reality as it presently exists. When you reach the rapids, no amount of resentment that "the water used to be calm, and it should still be calm" will help you negotiate through the rough waters and rocks. In fact, based on your inability to recognize reality immediately, as it presently exists, you might find yourself in the water or on the rocks.

On the other hand, if you continue to paddle as if you were still in the rapids when the raft reaches calm water, not only do you waste enormous amounts of energy but again you also may end up in the water or on the rocks.

Often current reality will be different from what you had expected. If you continually build up resentment at the disparity, then you are no longer fully in touch with current reality. An important ability in the creative process is the ability to recognize changes in reality as they occur.

UNWANTED SITUATIONS

A corporate executive scheduled an important meeting to improve overseas distribution of the company's electronic products. Two of the five company representatives from European countries were unable to attend as scheduled because of a sudden snowstorm in Europe which curtailed flights. The executive decided to hold the meeting without them. But he spent the entire time resenting the fact that the two representatives were not present. He even seemed to take out some of his resentment on the three who were there. He refused to recognize and accept current reality fully for what it was, which was that he was meeting with the three European representatives who could attend the meeting.

Because current reality often includes unwanted or unplanned-for situations, you may have a tendency to avoid accepting reality as it is. This nonacceptance disempowers you, for you cannot create the result you want based on a misrepresentation of current circumstances.

ANALYZING CURRENT REALITY

Some people avoid an accurate recognition of current reality by continually analyzing how current reality got to be the way it is. The question "How did things get to be the way they are?" is a different question from "What is presently going on?" Many people confuse the two questions, and so spend time futilely theorizing or explaining to themselves how they got to be where they are.

Les and Mary were driving to the Grand Canyon. That morning at the motel, they were told that the canyon was four hours away. After four hours of driving the Grand Canyon was nowhere in sight, and they were lost. Eventually they found a service station where they got directions. But for the hour and a half it took them to drive to the canyon from the service station they kept rehashing all the turns they had made, or not made, that had led them to the wrong place. And for the next half hour while they gazed at the Grand Canyon, they continued to analyze how they had gotten lost.

In the reactive-responsive orientation this kind of unproductive analysis is usually accompanied by the rationale that it does some good to find out how you got where you are. But the fact of the matter is that you are exactly where you are. Furthermore, rehashing how you got to where you are paradoxically has the function of obscuring where you are. In light of the creative process the conversation Les and Mary had was useless, for it did not help them in moving from the place where they were lost to the Grand Canyon.

If you find yourself repeatedly reviewing how you got to be where you are in your life, you are obscuring a clear view of current reality. Current reality is always your new starting point. To create the result they wanted, all that Les and Mary needed was a clear awareness of their new starting point, the place they wanted to be, and how best to get there.

The more directly and faster you can recognize current reality as it now is, the better. This ability is important especially when current reality turns out to be different from what you had expected. Developing this ability may take a little practice. But in the creative process, as you become more proficient in immediately recognizing shifts in current reality, you become better able to reorganize your approach spontaneously in a way that is consistent with the change in circumstances. You come to recognize even sudden and unexpected changes not as detrimental but rather as valuable and necessary feedback in the creative process.

Much successful psychotherapy is based on helping individuals have a greater acceptance of their current reality. Your mental health and emotional stability are directly affected by you recognizing your present state of affairs. This means telling yourself the truth about how things *really* are.

THE TRUTH ABOUT HOW THINGS ARE

Because avoiding discomfort is so valued in the reactive-responsive orientation, people often do not tell each other–and themselves–the full truth. Beginning from childhood, there is enormous presssure in society to collude in misrepresenting what is really occurring.

We tell children, "We don't have any more candy," when we know there is a drawer full of it. We misrepresent the truth when we say things like, "If you lie, your tongue will turn blue" or "Aunt

Sally isn't fat, she's just gained a few pounds" or "Dad and I aren't fighting, we're just having a discussion" or "Grandma's in the hospital, and we're sure she'll get better" (when we know she is dying). Elizabeth Kubler-Ross is rightfully outspoken about the harm done by parents lying to their children about death.

Socially accepted misrepresentation is designed primarily to protect people from feeling badly. When the waiter comes to our table and asks, "How was your dinner?" we tend to say, "Fine," even when we really want to say, "It was terrible."

The attempt to shelter people from the truth assumes that people cannot handle the full truth of reality. The fact is that almost everyone–including you–is much stronger, more resilient and more powerful than they are usually given credit for.

When you habitually misrepresent reality, the truth can seem dangerous to you.

The truth is not dangerous, it sets you free to create. It is only through your recognition of the facts of reality that you can engage the senior force of structural tension and move toward creating what really matters to you.

A PIVOTAL TECHNIQUE

Those moments when circumstances are not the way you would like them to be are actually very powerful and pivotal moments in the creative process. However wanted or unwanted your present circumstances may be, they function as needed feedback so that you can know the current status of the result you are creating.

Furthermore, times in which the situation or circumstances are not the way you want them to be are strategic moments because in those moments you are able to redefine what you want (your vision) and where you are (current reality) in such a way that both become clearer, and structural tension is strengthened.

A pivotal technique in the creative orientation may help you use unwanted circumstances as a catalyst to help propel you toward where you want to be. The technique is quite simple, yet profoundly powerful.

Step 1. Describe where you are. In other words, know exactly what the current reality is. If you are lost on your way to the Grand Canyon, report your circumstances to yourself factually, avoiding interpretation, analysis or editorial comment. "I am lost; I do not know in which direction the Grand Canyon lies. I am coming into a small town."

Step 2. Describe where you want to be. Spell out the result that you want to create. "I want to be at the Grand Canyon." Remember to separate what you want from what you think is possible, so that you are clearly in touch with what you want, and not limiting yourself in any way by what you think is possible under the circumstances.

Recall the test question: Would you take the result if you could have it? "If you could be at the Grand Canyon, would you take it?" If the answer is yes, then you want it.

Step 3. Once again, formally choose the result you want. Inwardly, say the words, "I choose . . ." adding the result you want ("I choose to be at the Grand Canyon").

Step 4. Move on. Once you have observed where you are, and where you want to be, and have formally chosen the result you want to create, change the focus of your conscious attention from being in an unwanted situation. Shift gears. Change the subject. You may look at the scenery, read a book, enjoy each other's company, or go back to what you were doing before you became focused on being lost or stuck. Les and Mary could have "moved on" by simply getting directions and then driving to the Grand Canyon.

Once when the great mathematician Henri Poincare was stuck trying to solve a complex equation, he took a nap. When he awoke, he had his answer. A famous chemical engineer seemed unable to find a formula to explain what he had discovered in the laboratory. He decided to take a ride around town on a bus. As he was stepping onto the bus, the solution came to him.

Author John Hyde Preston once asked Gertrude Stein:

But what if, when you tried to write, you felt stopped, suffocated, and no words came and if they came at all they were wooden and without meaning? What if you had the feeling you could never write another word?

Gertrude Stein replied, laughing:

Preston the way to resume is to resume. It is the only

way. To resume. If you feel this book deeply it will come as deep as your feeling is when it is running truest, and the book will never be truer or deeper than your feeling. But you do not yet know anything about your feeling because, though you may think it is all there, all crystallized, you have not let it run. So how can you know what it will be? What will be best in it is what you really do not know now. If you knew it all it would not be creation but dictation.

Perhaps you are typing an important letter, but things are not going well. You decide to use the pivotal technique. You realize your current reality (Step 1), you know what you want (Step 2), and you formally choose it (Step 3). To carry out Step 4, you may move on by doing something else, as the scientists did, or by resuming writing your letter. Moving on may include resuming the activity you were doing before you began this pivotal technique. As you move on, the structural tension you established in the first three steps is working organically to help you create the result.

MASTERING STRUCTURAL TENSION

Step 4 leaves the structural tension unresolved. This is very desirable, because then you are able to assimilate the structural tension more easily. The tension will be particularly helpful in generating natural processes in which the path of least resistance leads you directly toward the result. The natural tendency of tension is to move toward resolution. The natural structural tendency is for all the resources available to you, known and unknown, to reorganize themselves organically in ways which resolve the tension you established by doing the first three steps.

One of the great secrets in the art of creating is mastering the force of structural tension. If you attempt prematurely to resolve the tension you have established, you weaken your ability to create the results you want.

Masters of structural tension know how to generate the latent forces which enable them to establish a powerfully dynamic structure.

Martin Luther King, Jr. had the ability to observe current reality objectively yet compassionately, and simultaneously hold a vision of freedom and justice. In his great "I have a dream" speech, he established a clear view of current reality and an equally clear view of a nation which "rises up and lives out the true meaning of its creed" of freedom and justice.

People like King know that in this structure the path of least resistance leads most directly to the results they are creating.

Years ago I was trying to use a hand saw to cut a piece of wood. A friend who was a skilled carpenter came by as I was struggling ineffectively with the saw. He smiled and said, "Let your tool do the job it was designed to do." He then showed me how to use the hand saw properly, and I was able to finish my project using only a fraction of my original effort.

In a similar way, instead of trying to force yourself to resolve the tension created by the discrepancy between current reality and your vision, let structural tension do the job it was designed to do. As a creator, even in an unwanted situation you learn to establish tension and hold that tension until it is organically resolved.

The organic process by which you move to where you want to be may include conventional or new approaches. But these approaches will be natural expressions of the path of least resistance generated by the structural tension you established, and therefore they will be the most effective and direct route to creating your vision.

APPLYING THE PIVOTAL TECHNIQUE

How might the executive concerned about his overseas distribution have used the pivotal technique in the unwanted situation in which two of the five company representatives were snowbound in Europe? Let us go through the four steps for him.

Step 1 is to describe current reality. The executive might have described his situation this way: "A meeting, which was to involve five European representatives vital to my company's overseas distribution, can be attended by only three of them."

This would seem to be an adequate description of his current reality. To create structural tension, it is necessary to have a clear representation only of the facts of current reality; theories, explanations, apologies and other embellishments of the facts are not necessary. Particularly *un*important in his description of current reality would be a statement of the reason two representatives were not present.

Step 2 is to describe the result you want to create. The executive might have described the result he wanted to create as "a fully attended meeting, with all five representatives present."

Would this actually have described what he wanted?. Sometimes this step can be a little tricky. Upon reflection, it would become clear that he was actually describing not the result he wanted to create but *the process he had originally designed* to get what he wanted. If what he had set out to do was only to have a fully attended meeting, he would not have been able to establish effective structural tension which would have led him to the ultimate result he wanted to create. Why? Because he failed to be clear about the result he really wanted.

What did he really want? We might have discovered from questioning him that the result he actually wanted was "exceptional overseas distribution of his company's product." The meeting with his overseas representatives was only part of a process designed to help accomplish this result. The result he truly wanted was quite different from what he first thought. Now that he knew the result he wanted, his vision could be described as "exceptional overseas distribution."

His now clarified vision of what he wanted to create, however, would modify what was relevant in his description of current reality. If exceptional overseas distribution was the vision, what was the current reality about overseas distribution? At this point, he would need to revise step one of the pivotal technique.

Step one is to describe current reality. At the time of the meeting, the executive's current reality was that the overseas distribution of the company's products was inadequate. Shipments arrived at local distribution points after long delivery delays. Because of these delays, many of the local European outlets found it difficult to satisfy their customers. Adequate shipments of the product were being sent from the United States to Europe; the delays were happening after the shipments arrived in Europe. For the executive, this would be an adequate description of current reality. Based on this picture, the executive would be able to clarify his vision.

In carrying out step two of the pivotal technique, the executive would describe the result he wanted as "an exceptional overseas distribution, which includes local European outlets receiving our products within thirty days of their orders."

At this point in the technique, the executive would be careful to avoid getting involved in considerations of whether or not this result was possible. At this point, he would simply not know whether his vision was possible. He would only know—and would only need to know—that this was the result he wanted. Furthermore, in his mind the result would be seen clearly enough so that he would be able to recognize it if it occurred.

The final test to see whether or not this was a result he wanted would be his answer to the question: "If you could have exceptional overseas distribution with thirty-day delivery service, would you take it?" His answer would probably be yes. Therefore, this was a result he wanted, and he would be ready to move to the next step.

Step 3 is formally to choose the result you want to create. Inwardly, he might formally choose it by saying, "I choose to have exceptional overseas distribution of our company's product, with thirty-day delivery service."

Step 4 is to move on. The executive might do this by conducting his meeting with the three attending European representatives. By moving on in this way, he would allow the structural tension between where he was (inadequate distribution) and where he wanted to be (exceptional distribution) to exist. He would further allow an organic process to take place, in which the path of least resistance would lead toward "exceptional distribution."

In this context, the meeting with the three representatives would take on an entirely new meaning for the executive. First of all, the meeting's own highest potential as a step in the process toward the result he wanted to create would tend to be realized, whatever that might be. Second, the meeting itself might or might not directly contribute to the result of exceptional distribution of the product. But it would not really matter, for the executive would be able to invent whatever processes were needed to accomplish the result. He would be able to do this organically, so that not only would conventional methods become available, but also new ones that had never before occurred to him.

THE ETHICS OF THE CREATIVE PROCESS

In the orientation of the creative you are never in the position of violating your own moral, spiritual, or ethical standards, because one of the results you create in shifting to this orientation is "you being true to that which is highest in you." The executive would not only generate effective procedures for producing the exceptional overseas distribution that he wanted, but he would do so within the framework of being true to himself. He would never find himself in the position of justifying wrong means to a right end, because right means–ones which are consistent with what is highest in the human spirit–are the most effective means. They are the ones organically generated from the structure, and they allow you to follow the path of least resistance to the desired result.

In fact, the only time people use processes which violate their moral or ethical standards is when they are in the reactive-responsive orientation, where the assumption of powerlessness permeates the structure. At times, persons in the reactive-responsive orientation attempt to compensate for powerlessness by compromising themselves "because the circumstances require it."

Each moment in life is part of a structure. Included in that structure is always the potential to bring forth the highest good. This potential is not at all a matter of attitude–for example, thinking positively–but rather a matter of the highest good being evoked by an act of creation.

Therefore all moments, but especially those moments which seem difficult, troublesome, problematic or hopeless, are moments of great creative power in your life. The "difficult, problematic" moments are, in fact, strategic moments which can help you bring the creative process to completion.

CHAPTER 17

COMPLETION

THE THIRD STAGE OF THE CREATIVE CYCLE

Completion, the third and final stage of the creative cycle, is the full and total accomplishment of the result you want to create. When this stage is finished, you have successfully created your vision.

"PRISONER SYNDROME"

Shortly before prisoners are to be released, they often experience sleepless nights, anxiety, loss of appetite, and a host of other unpleasant feelings. This experience comes, paradoxically, after years of looking forward to the day when they will be released.

For many people, this kind of anticipatory anxiety can exist on a much subtler level. For example, as we have seen from observing structural conflict in people who want a good relationship, the closer they get to having what they desire, the more pull there is in the opposite direction. Often, the path of least resistance leads them away from the relationship they want.

THE EXPERIENCE OF COMPLETION

There are two common experiences people associate with having what they want or with anything coming to completion.

One experience is of fulfillment and satisfaction.

The other common experience is of depression and loss, as in *"post partum* blues," the depression women sometimes experience after successfully completing the process of childbirth. The prisoners about to be released were also having this uncomfortable kind of reaction.

Since many people associate uncomfortable emotional experiences with completion, and they have a tendency to avoid such emotional discomfort, they also often have a tendency to avoid successful completion itself.

In the creative cycle, completion is a unique and separate stage, and has its own requirements to be mastered.

THE ABILITY TO RECEIVE

One of the major abilities to be developed at this stage is the ability to receive the full fruits of your labor.

Some years ago I became conscious of my own inability to receive fully. I was beginning to accomplish the results I had been working on, in some cases for years. My relationships with people I cared about were deeply satisfying, the DMA organization was becoming more and more successful, the approaches to growth and development I was creating were directly useful to many people, and I was living in the town where I had dreamed of living ever since I was a teenager. Even though I was glad to see in reality all these things that I had envisioned for so long, I also felt somewhat strange. The more results I was accomplishing the stronger this strange feeling grew.

I examined what was going on, and realized that I had not learned to receive. I had not been allowing myself fully to have the results I had worked for so many years to create. Once I realized that I was inadequately receiving those results, I took it upon myself to learn to accept and fully receive them, for I saw clearly that receiving was an essential part of the creative process.

Receiving is a very simple process. When the United Parcel Service carrier delivers a package to you, you receive the package by accepting it from him. But until you accept it, you don't have the package. If you are unable to receive what you are creating, you are stopping short of completion. Until you fully accept the results into your life, the results are not fully created. You don't have the package.

[143   ]

GIVING AND RECEIVING

Many people with whom I work have a natural desire to serve. In a sense, they are experts at giving. However, they are often inept at receiving. Many who spend much of their lives supporting others have not developed the ability to receive. There is nothing altruistic about your inability to receive well, for no one is served any better by your inability to receive. If anything, it only teaches the people being served by you how *not* to receive the service you are giving them.

The structural conflict most common in dysfunctional life patterns involves the dominant belief that you cannot have what you really want. When you believe that it is somehow wrong or not possible for you to receive fully what you want or what matters most to you–and yet there is something you want–you are in a structural conflict.

In the reactive-responsive orientation, the structural conflict (generated by this belief, on the one side, and your aspiration, on the other) gives rise to a path of least resistance leading you away from receiving what you want whenever you get close to receiving it.

Alchemists of old sought to turn lead into gold. Many people in the reactive-responsive orientation, where structural conflict is the dominant structure, have a talent for reverse alchemy: turning gold into lead.

Once you have made the shift to the orientation of the creative, where the senior force of structural tension supersedes structural conflict, receiving what has been created becomes natural and familiar. While at first it may be an unusual and unfamiliar experience to have what you want, in time having what you want becomes relatively easy to live with.

COMPLETION AND ACKNOWLEDGMENT

According to the Judeo-Christian tradition, as expressed in the opening chapter of the book of *Genesis*, human beings are made in the image and likeness of God. Since the first description of God in the Bible is as a creator, humans made in the image and likeness of a creator are made to be creators.

Not only does *Genesis* imply that we are creators, but the story of Creation reveals the universal structure of the creative cycle. The stages described in *Genesis* for each day of creation include germination, assimilation, and completion. Germination is initiated in a sequence of choices made by God: "Let there be light," "Let the waters be gathered together," "Let the dry land appear," and so on. Assimilation happens as the results form themselves into their full manifestation, as described in the text. Completion occurs when God declares that the results created are good, for example, "And God saw that the light was good."

The repeated declaration, "And God saw that it was good" is an act of acknowledgment. Each day of creation had its own acknowledgment. In the creative process, acknowledging the steps you have taken toward your goal is an important act of completion.

ACKNOWLEDGING WHAT YOU HAVE CREATED

Acknowledging the results you have created is a different act from receiving those results into your life. Receiving is an incoming action: you accept into your life what you have created. Acknowledging is an outgoing action: you bestow your judgment upon the results. You judge the results as being complete. When an artist signs a painting, he or she acknowledges the painting and judges it as being complete.

In light of structural tension, when you acknowledge results as being fully or partly created, you are recognizing an important aspect of your current reality: the fact that it is changing and moving in the direction of your vision. Furthermore, in light of the creative cycle, acknowledging the results you have created establishes more deeply the fact that you are in the stage of completion.

In the reactive-responsive orientation the step of acknowledgment is most often neglected. If you are either reacting or responding to circumstantial stimuli, then the power in your life is assumed to be in the circumstances rather than in you. Your "acknowledgment" that a desired result has been achieved means little, since you see the result as coming about more from the good graces of the circumstances (good luck) than by your own creation. You can hardly sign your name to it.

In the orientation of the creative, you are the only one who is able to declare a result complete, for it is you alone who determine when reality satisfies your vision.

If you are creating a painting, at what point is the painting complete? This is an important question, since it is always possible to add more details or to change the painting in other ways. You determine that the painting is finished by your recognition that the painting satisfies your vision of it. In other words, current reality matches your vision of the result. You are the only one who can make the judgment that the painting is finished.

In the creative orientation, judgment of this kind is essential. A notion recently in vogue was that people should avoid being judgmental. However, making judgments about the status of results you are creating is a necessary part of creating them.

As Charles Krauthammer observed in an astute *TIME* essay,

> . . . perhaps the deepest cause of moral confusion is the state of language itself, language that has been bleached of its moral distinctions, turned neutral, value-free, "nonjudgmental." When that happens, moral discourse becomes difficult, moral distinctions impossible and moral debate incomprehensible . . . . The trouble with blurring moral distinctions, even for the best of causes, is that it can become a habit. It is a habit we can ill afford, since the modern tolerance for such distinctions is already in decline. Some serious ideas are used so promiscuously in the service of so many causes that they have lost all their power. Genocide, for example, has been used to describe almost every kind of perceived injustice, from Viet Nam to pornography to Third World birth control. A new word, holocaust, has to be brought in as a substitute. But its life before ultimate trivialization will not be long. Only last month a financial commentator on PBS, referring to a stock-market drop, spoke of the holocaust year of 1981. The host did not blink.

In the reactive-responsive orientation, the fashion of avoiding distinctions and judgments is designed to minimize the experience of conflict. In the creative orientation, making judgments is essential, and the ability to make significant distinctions is one of the prerequisites of the creative process.

SEEKING "ACKNOWLEDGMENT"

Many people in the reactive-responsive orientation seek "acknowledgment" or praise for the work that they do. This kind of acknowledgment–in which their ability to feel good about themselves and what they are doing depends on the circumstance of having other people approve of them–is very different from the kind of acknowledgment we have been discussing.

In the creative orientation what matters is not how *you* are doing but rather how close your vision–*what you want to create*–is to being realized. A thousand people could praise a result you had created, but if the result did not satisfy your vision, you would not be ready to acknowledge it as complete. On the other hand, a thousand people might condemn a result you had created, yet if you saw that it satisfied your vision you would be fully ready to say "that it was good." As the predominant creative force in your life, only you have the authority to recognize and confirm a result as complete.

THE ENERGY OF COMPLETION

When you make this acknowledgment, you enable the very special energy of completion to be released. One function of this energy is to propel you toward the germination of a new creative cycle. Each time you complete an act of creation, you focus a life force. And since life begets life, this energy seeks to enlarge and expand its expression through new creation. In the stage of completion, your being is ready for another act of creation.

Your life can be a series of creative acts which beget other creative acts.

Whenever I walk through any city, no matter what the crime rate or political corruption, no matter if overpopulation or environmental problems exist, I am struck by the fact that there is vastly more human energy being directed toward building our civilization than toward any other goal.

Humans are creative beings. Our natural instincts, desires and tendencies are toward creating. Our general aspirations as a species, including both Eastern and Western civilizations, are most naturally toward building, creating, constructing, inventing, forming, improving, structuring, shaping that which we truly want.

In the prophetic words of John F. Kennedy during his Inaugural Address,

> The times are different now
> For man holds in his mortal hands
> The power to obliterate
> all forms of human misery
> and all forms of human life.

As human society, we hold in our hands the power to live life on the planet any way we choose. This power is our birthright. It can neither be granted to us nor taken away from us.

HUMAN DESTINY AND PURPOSE

As an individual, only you can be the final authority on how you use—or fail to use—this power. Hence, your individual destiny is in your own hands.

No matter how difficult you may claim your circumstances are, there are individuals who have been in even more difficult circumstances and yet have created their lives in accordance with what truly mattered to them.

Christy Brown, a quadriplegic who could only move a few of his toes and his mouth, became a good painter and a great writer. Beethoven, perhaps the greatest composer, was deaf. Leonardo da Vinci suffered all his life from dyslexia.

You are never the victim of your circumstances. These circumstances are simply part of the raw material of the creative process.

Learning to create is very natural. Even mastering your own creative process is no different in that way from learning to walk or talk. But since so little emphasis has been placed on creating as a

[148]

way of life, few people in our society, up to now, have mastered it.

The instinct to create does not go away. It seeks expression. When you create, you align yourself with your most natural state of being. As a consequence, many of the difficulties of your life either disappear or are no longer important issues for you. In the orientation of the creative the physical, mental, emotional, and spiritual dimensions of your being realign themselves and work in harmony. Based on their realignment, the path of least resistance in your life leads you toward fulfilling your deepest and most profound life purpose.

PART THREE: MANIPULATION, MASTERY,
AND TRANSCENDENCE

CHAPTER 18

CONFLICT MANIPULATION

WORRY AS A STRATEGY

How much do you worry?

If you worry chronically, what you are doing is presenting your-self with a negative vision–the vision of circumstances as they might occur at their worst.

As we have seen, the path of least resistance in a structural conflict leads you back and forth between two mutually exclusive points of resolution. Worry is a strategy designed to increase the intensity of the structural conflict so much that you will be "moti-vated" to take action–action designed to avoid the negative conse-quences you envision. The problem, as chronic worriers see it, is that unless they worry intensely enough they will not take action.

Chronic worriers keep high pressure on themselves. They at-tempt to mobilize themselves into action by reminding themselves of all that could go wrong. In reaction to the buildup of worry and conflict, they control themselves and force themselves to take action in order to avoid getting something they do not want. The action they take, as in all reaction or response to structural conflict, is an attempt to resolve an unresolvable conflict.

A CLASSIC CASE OF MANIPULATIVE STRATEGY

Like many other people, Henry always waits until the very last minute to do things. Henry had three days left before the deadline to have his car inspected. During those days, he imagined everything that might be wrong with his car and thought of all the reasons why his car might not pass the test. He reviewed each potential problem over and over in his mind, each time with increasing anxiety. He also imagined his car failing the inspection. If it did not pass inspection, he would not be able to drive his car until it met state standards. He envisioned his car in the repairshop for days. Without his car, it would be very difficult for Henry to carry on his sales work, since much of it involved driving.

During this time, Henry was building up his anxiety. When he finally drove his car into the inspection garage, he did so much more as an attempt to relieve the emotional pressure he had put upon himself than to see whether or not he had a car which met state requirements. Henry's buildup of worry and conflict was a strategy he used on himself, designed to force him to bring his car in for inspection.

In the reactive-responsive orientation, this type of avoidance strategy is the most common form of manipulation used to deal with structural conflict. In its general form, it is called *conflict manipulation*. It is an attempt to intensify a structural conflict in order to manipulate yourself to do things or to manipulate someone else to get things done on your behalf.

HOW CONFLICT MANIPULATION WORKS

If you wanted for some reason to engage in conflict manipulation, how would you proceed?

Conflict manipulation begins when there is a structural conflict which is dominant. In Henry's case the dominant structural conflict was the following: on the one hand, Henry wanted his car to pass inspection; on the other, he had a dominant belief that "Left to my own devices, I won't get around to doing what needs to be done," specifically, bringing the car in for inspection.

Step one. When a structural conflict is dominant in you, build up emotional conflict by presenting yourself with visions of unwanted and undesirable consequences. Look for the worst potential in the situation. Here, Henry envisioned failing the inspection, not being able to use his car, having lots of repair bills, losing money by missing sales contacts, and so on.

Step two. When the state of emotional conflict becomes intolerable, take action. For Henry, it was getting his car to the inspection station. Usually, the actions taken appear to be some form of problem-solving or some way of avoiding negative consequences. But structurally the purpose of these actions is to relieve exacerbated emotional conflict. Within the structure of conflict manipulation, at this stage the path of least resistance leads you to take action designed to relieve the emotional pressure.

THE AREA OF TOLERANCE

Structurally, the actions taken in conflict manipulation have an *internal* reference point (how Henry feels) rather than an *external* one (Henry's car passing or not passing inspection). This form of manipulation relies on internal standards of emotional tolerance.

In the reactive-responsive orientation, a person in a structural conflict has an area of tolerance outside of which he or she will not feel comfortable.

In Chapter 4, Structural Conflict, I figuratively described persons in structual conflict as having two giant rubber bands around the waist pulling in opposite directions. The farther they move in one direction, the more pull there is from the opposite direction. In this structure, the path of least resistance leads them in the direction of the strongest pull, but as they move in that direction the pull from the opposite direction increases and they move back again, and so on.

At what point do they shift direction? For different people there are different points, because they have different degrees of tolerance. The point at which a person shifts direction marks the outer limit of their area of tolerance of discomfort.

If Henry were to take one more step beyond his area of tolerance, he would feel pronounced discomfort. So usually he shifts direction before he passes the outer limit of his area of tolerance.

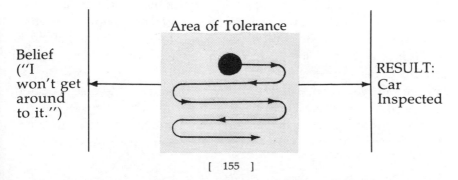

In the conflict manipulation strategy which Henry utilizes to get his car inspected, however, he pushes himself out beyond the boundary of his area of tolerance. He does this by building up emotional conflict in himself (step one), envisioning all the negative results which might happen if he took his car to the inspection station. Notice that as he intensifies his emotional conflict, he is pushing himself toward a vision of undesirable consequences; this starts him moving in the opposite direction from where he wants to end up. As he pushes in that direction, however, he continues to build up tension in the rubber band attached to the opposite result (getting the car inspected). He stretches this rubber band so much that he is then propelled, as if shot from a sling, toward getting his car inspected. And in this way he is able to take the action (step two).

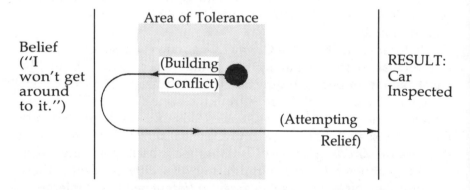

Structurally, in this form of manipulation, the buildup of emotional conflict has only one actual goal: emotional relief. Henry brought his car to be inspected motivated primarily by the need for emotional relief from the conflict he himself had produced. Henry was using a manipulative strategy typical of the reactive-responsive orientation. He actually did get his car inspected, but he used extreme measures to accomplish it. Not only did the process take a toll on him emotionally and physically, but it also reinforced his belief that he is powerless and that, left to his own devices, he would never get around to doing things.

In Henry's mind, he was forced into getting his car inspected by the circumstances, which were a direct threat to him. It was the circumstances–the state inspection law, the deadline, etc.–that got his car inspected. It certainly was not a secondary choice he easily made to support a primary choice of having a legally registered car.

A POPULAR STRATEGY

There are many applications of conflict manipulation in the re-active-responsive orientation. This strategy is used in human relationships, in breaking habits, in overcoming addictions, and in promoting community causes.

In whatever variation it is used, this strategy of conflict manipulation has serious drawbacks. First, as we saw with Henry, such manipulation undermines your relationship with yourself. Second, each time you use this manipulative strategy, you reinforce your experience of powerlessness, so that you become less and less able to create what you want.

You may discover that you actually employ this strategy more often than you think. Henry used this strategy not only in getting his car inspected. It was the strategy he used to get himself to file his income tax, keep appointments with his dentist, keep his weight down, and get to work on time. Even projects at work got finished mostly through self-manipulation. This was his common way of doing things.

CONFLICT MANIPULATION IN HUMAN INTERACTION

While Henry primarily directed conflict manipulation toward himself, in a form of self-manipulation, often conflict manipulation is directed primarily toward others.

Linda was having trouble getting her fourteen-year-old son Randy to study. All he seemed interested in were videogames and *Dungeons and Dragons*, which he played for hours. Linda used conflict manipulation on Randy by warning him about the negative consequences of not doing well in school. She began by telling him how difficult it would be for him to get into college. When that did not seem to build enough conflict in Randy (to "motivate" him) to get him away from his games, she cautioned him that everyone would think he was stupid. When that had no effect she began to tell Randy how badly he made her feel. This tactic did not seem to produce the desired result, so Linda began to yell at him, attempting to pressure him with her anger.

Linda's strategy was to get Randy to experience emotional conflict intensely enough so that he would change his behavior. When her first approach failed to work, she moved to a more intense form of negative vision. She then attempted to increase his conflict, through guilt, by telling him how badly he made her feel. Her final ploy was to get angry and shout.

In this particular case, Randy had learned how to ignore his mother's attempts to produce conflict in him. He did this through some conflict manipulation of his own. In order to avoid his own inner experience of emotional conflict, he forced himself to remain untouched by her.

With Randy and his mother, conflict manipulation remained incomplete. It did not go beyond step one (buildup of emotional conflict), because Linda was never able to increase Randy's conflict to an intolerable level.

Often in human interactions, however, both steps of conflict manipulation—intensification of conflict and action to reduce emotional discomfort—are completed.

Paul was continually telling his friend Pam that if she did not eat "health foods" she would be susceptible to serious illness. At first Pam did not take Paul seriously. But he continued to attempt to demonstrate that her diet was dangerous by showing her articles from his health magazines about people who had attributed various types of cancer, heart disease, diabetes, and arthritis to eating unhealthy foods. Every time they had a meal together Paul would remind Pam of his opinion about her eating habits. Pam began to feel more and more emotional conflict every time Paul mentioned food, which he did quite often. Eventually, all Pam had to do was look at food and she would begin to wonder if she was going to develop some awful illness.

She finally began to follow the diet Paul was promoting. She was eating health foods not because she thought they would bring her into a state of greater health, and not even to avoid the terrible illnesses Paul was describing, but primarily to relieve the pressure of her emotional anxiety. In other words, her path of least resistance led her to begin eating health food in order to restore emotional equilibrium.

While Paul might have had good intentions in attempting to get Pam to accept his beliefs about health foods, both he and Pam were actually engaged in conflict manipulation. Paul performed step one by increasing Pam's emotional conflict. Pam carried out step two by taking action attempting to relieve her emotional distress.

SHORT-LIVED EFFECTS

Pam began to revert to her old eating habits as soon as the pressure was off. Because she had changed her diet primarily to relieve her emotional discomfort, her motivation to eat health foods vanished as soon as her emotional state became more comfortable.

Another outcome of Paul's attempt to manipulate Pam into eating health foods was that their relationship became strained. Pam had built up resentment about Paul's imposition of his beliefs on her. To Pam, Paul began to symbolize a source of emotional conflict, so that when they were together Pam felt she was unable to be herself fully.

Because conflict manipulation includes building up an emotional conflict and then taking action designed to relieve it, the actions taken almost never have any real and lasting effects. If action taken actually reduces the emotional conflict (as Pam's beginning to eat health foods did), the conflict itself is reduced. Once the conflict is reduced, however, there is less pressure to maintain the new action. And once there is less pressure to act in this way, the path of least resistance leads to a return to former habits (as when Pam returned to her former diet).

This series of steps occurs because the structure of conflict manipulation has a built-in "compensation factor": as you put pressure upon the structure by increasing the conflict, the structure compensates by pushing back, through action, to reduce the pressure. Once the pressure is reduced, the structure returns to its former state.

BREAKING HABITS THROUGH
CONFLICT MANIPULATION

A popular approach in trying to change destructive habits such as overeating, alcohol or drug abuse, gambling, smoking, etc., is to use variations of conflict manipulation. The two basic steps, however, remain the same.

Step one of conflict manipulation is to intensify or exacerbate the conflict. In attempting to break bad habits this step is usually carried out by presenting vivid negative visions of a life filled with terrible consequences which are a result of your bad habit, the one you are trying to break.

Step two, in general, is to take action designed to relieve the emotional conflict that was set up in step one. In the case of breaking a habit, the action that is taken at this point is to stop or reduce the unwanted habit.

As many experts on addiction know, the first few attempts to employ conflict manipulation usually end up with the addicted person returning to the unwanted habit. This happens because of the way the structure works. When the conflict set up in step one is lessened by temporarily stopping the habit in step two, the path of least resistance leads the addicted person back to the original habit.

Eventually, in response to such "failures," those using conflict manipulation often move to the strategy of never letting the conflict reduce in intensity. Thus, step one is always being applied. There is never any let up. Alcoholics continue to tell each other that they will always be alcoholics and that at any moment they may revert to drinking, no matter how many years they have been on the wagon. Similarly, in some programs designed to help people stop overeating participants are trained to warn themselves continually that they are powerless and uncontrollable and, therefore, must at all costs keep a close watch on themselves. If they do not, they are told, they will overeat.

In the reactive-responsive orientation, since the power in life is assumed to be in the circumstantial stimuli, it seems as if the only alternatives addicted people have are either to remain addicted or to engage continuously in conflict manipulation, in which case they continually exacerbate emotional conflict in order to keep from drinking, gambling, overeating, etc.

If those were the only choices for addicted persons, then certainly in most cases conflict manipulation would be the better of the two alternatives since most addictions have direct detrimental physical and emotional consequences.

However, whether or not a person drinks or does not drink,

uses drugs or doesn't, overeats or does not overeat, no real change happens in the basic underlying structure in the addicted person's life through the use of strategies based on conflict manipulation. For why do you suppose they drink or overeat or take drugs or smoke in the first place? Structurally, these habitual actions themselves are taken as an attempt to reduce various kinds of emotional distress that the addicted person experiences. Such conflicts may involve deep loss, grief, fear, guilt, and the like. The strategy to break an addictive habit is generally to make the conflict over the habit more dominant than the distress which it is an attempt to resolve (loss, grief, fear, guilt, and so on).

In William Glasser's book *Positive Addiction*, certain non-disruptive habits such as meditation, jogging, yoga, and other forms of exercise are shown to be useful substitutes for negative addictions.

A man who had been an alcoholic for seventeen years was able to substitute an hour of daily meditation for his drinking habit. For him, meditation became a positive addiction. When asked what happens on days when he doesn't meditate, he described physiological symptoms similar to those he previously experienced when attempting to withdraw from alcohol, except that his present symptoms were due to withdrawal from meditation.

The underlying structure of positive addiction is the same as that of negative addiction. While a positive addiction is much healthier than a negative one, an undermining effect still occurs. For the addiction itself, whether positive or negative, is a strategy to avoid the negative, unwanted consequences of the withdrawal symptoms. In one way or another, the addicted person is living in a state of manipulation. This is not always necessary.

Stanton Peele, a recognized expert on addictions, contends that the best way to stop an unwanted habit or an addiction is simply to stop it. He believes that is what most people actually do. He cites case studies which contradict the common notion that addictions are very difficult to stop.

For example, 95 percent of the soldiers who were addicted to heroin in Viet Nam were able to end their use of heroin easily when they returned to the United States. Furthermore, 85 percent of those who were classified as *seriously* addicted were able to quit easily when they returned home. Based on common notions about drug addiction, experts had been predicting epidemics of heroin addiction when these servicemen returned to the United States. But the epidemics never materialized. Why not?

Peele proposes the answer that these servicemen–and people in general–have much more capacity for self-reliance than they are given credit for. He further suggests that many of the experts dealing with addiction use approaches which undermine the individual's self-reliance, thus making it more difficult rather than less difficult for their clients to change unwanted habits.

As we have seen, many "expert" approaches to breaking addictive habits employ conflict manipulation, a strategy limited in its ability to effect real and lasting change. While there can be some observable change at the behavioral level, such a strategy, overall, tends to undermine self-reliance and to reinforce a sense of powerlessness in the individual, so that the crutch of conflict manipulation must be used again and again. This is because the underlying reactive-responsive structure remains unchanged.

When a real change in the underlying structure occurs, as in the shift to the orientation of the creative, it is possible for the path of least resistance to lead directly toward what you want. As part of following that path, unwanted habits which might interfere with what you really want often change automatically. Sometimes, as part of the organic creative process, it may be necessary to make secondary choices to support your primary choices. But making secondary choices in support of what you want is very different from action taken as a step in conflict manipulation.

The potential always exists for people to reach far beyond their present circumstances–but not through the strategy of conflict manipulation.

NEGATIVE VISIONS: FEAR, GUILT, AND PITY

Conflict manipulation has become a popular strategy in promoting and fundraising for a number of community causes–social, health, political, religious, etc. At one time or another they all employ the same formula, though some manipulate through fear while others use guilt and pity.

Organizations formed around fighting cancer attempt to scare you into quitting smoking or eating certain foods by threatening you with a vision of cancer.

The heart societies try to get you to follow low-cholesterol, salt-free diets by threatening you with a vision of a heart attack.

Every day hundreds of radio evangelists promote a vision of evil in an attempt to scare you into being good.

The anti-nuclear movement promotes a frightening vision of planetary holocaust in an attempt to scare you into social action against nuclear weapons.

The Pentagon, ironically, uses the same form of conflict manipulation by promoting a frightening vision of Soviet nuclear attack in an attempt to scare you into funding a nuclear weapons buildup.

Environmentalists attempt to scare you into supporting environmental regulation by promoting dire visions of acid rain and polluted waters while at the same time, using the same strategy, some business and political leaders attempt to scare you into supporting environmental deregulation by promoting a dire vision of a ruined economy and widespread high unemployment.

The "moral majority" attempts to scare you into voting for their candidates by promoting a vision of amoral and unpatriotic office-holders.

Using the emotions of guilt and pity, certain hunger-relief organizations attempt to gain your support by promoting visions of starving children. Certain disaster-relief organizations attempt to gain your support by promoting visions of human misery.

Equal rights and civil rights organizations attempt to enlist your support, often through guilt, by promoting visions of injustice, racism, hate, sexism, and prejudice.

Groups organized to protect endangered species induce a combination of guilt and pity by promoting a vision of the slaughter of whales, seals, and other forms of wildlife, so that you will send money and support their causes.

The great irony is that each one of these groups, by using conflict manipulation, promotes a negative vision–a vision which is, in most cases, the opposite of what they really want to see manifested on the planet. One tragedy of our times is that well-meaning people often lend enormous amounts of energy to those visions that they really do not want to see happen.

CONFLICT MANIPULATION AND POWERLESSNESS

Since conflict manipulation involves operating within the reactive-responsive orientation, and hence reinforcing that orientation, conflict manipulation also reinforces the experience of powerlessness. Building a new and better civilization is impossible, when it is based on powerlessness.

Current reality does, in fact, include cancer and other serious health problems, hunger and starvation, excessive armaments and wars, cruelty and misery, environmental imbalance and endangered species, sexism and other prejudice, terrorism and fanaticism.

Many of these situations are caused, fundamentally, by people's chronic experience of powerlessness; others, while not the direct results of such powerlessness, are aggravated by it. Attempting to change situations which have their roots in powerlessness through a strategy which reinforces powerlessness is folly.

Powerlessness is a primary characteristic of the reactive-responsive orientation. The more powerlessness is expressed on the planet, the less able people are to shape their destinies. The more powerless a society becomes, the more it tends toward extremism. The more extreme it grows, the more reactive it becomes. The more reactive, the more destructive—even self-destructive.

Finding "solutions" to our problems—a reactive-responsive approach—is no solution. The major world dilemma we are faced with today is that we are living with a fundamental orientation (the reactive-responsive) in which any attempts to improve society by means of that orientation can only reinforce and deepen that orientation, thus making matters worse.

Rather than a world trying to solve its problems by reacting or responding to them, it is possible to have a world that is focused on creating what we truly want. We can shift to an orientation motivated not by powerlessness, fear, guilt, pity, empty sentimentality or self-indulgence, but by aspiration toward that which is highest, a challenge worthy of society, a manifestation of natural human goodness, unconditional love and compassion, and a vision of the planet in which the human spirit is fulfilled.

CHAPTER 19

WILLPOWER MANIPULATION

WILLPOWER AND THE REACTIVE-RESPONSIVE ORIENTATION

Every year, thousands of books and magazine articles are written in one way or another encouraging people to develop their willpower. A common misconception, which originates in the reactive-responsive orientation, is that willpower is needed to accomplish most things. In fact, it is not.

The use of "willpower" is a strategy designed to overpower yourself. In expressing willpower, you are attempting to force yourself into compliance with what you wish to see happen. If you succeed, you are considered strong-willed; if you fail, you are considered weak-willed.

The message, prevalent in the reactive-responsive orientation, is that people need somehow to generate volition and intention–to "motivate" themselves–in order to make things happen. Most people feel they never have enough willpower to accomplish anything significant. Nevertheless, people often attempt to use willpower. In the reactive-responsive orientation, they employ it in a strategy designed to overcome structural conflict. I call this strategy *willpower manipulation*.

Willpower manipulation uses a strategy different from the strategy of conflict manipulation, though both are designed to overcome structural conflict.

Let us say you want a certain result, but you have a dominant belief that you cannot have it (structural conflict). In conflict manipulation, the focus is on negative consequences of not acting, and the strategy is to build up an emotional conflict over the negative consequences to such an intolerable intensity that you are propelled backward toward taking action to carry out what you want to see happen. This is what Henry did to get himself to take his car in for inspection, and what Linda attempted to do to get her son to do his homework.

On the other hand, in willpower manipulation you do not intensify the emotional conflict about the belief that you cannot have what you want, but rather use a strategy which attempts to overpower that belief by exerting what is supposed to be a greater force than the belief, namely, your willpower. Often this strategy takes the form of *intensifying the belief you have in the power of your will.*

Among those in the reactive-responsive orientation, building up willpower often takes the form of developing "positive" attitudes or strong "intention."

POSITIVE ATTITUDES

For years, advocates of positive thinking have claimed that your attitudes will shape your destiny, and that if you think positive thoughts, positive results will occur. The strategy you use to think positive thoughts is to force yourself into thinking the "best" of any situation. This is true for both common approaches to positive thinking. Both approaches use willpower manipulation.

If you wake up in the morning and you feel sick, tired, and headachy, one school of positive thinking would have you force yourself to think something like, "Boy, I feel great today. Isn't it fabulous to be alive?"

A second school of positive thinking would have you say to yourself something like, "I really feel sick. I think it's just wonderful that I feel sick, because good things always come from these kinds of situations."

In a situation like this, whenever you attempt to impose upon yourself a predetermined attitude or thought pattern, you are cutting yourself off from a clear, accurate, and objective view of current reality and, therefore, disempowering yourself.

Positive thinking is a willpower strategy designed to help people exert their will over themselves as a kind of self-manipulation.

There are two assumptions, generally unexpressed and unexamined, at the roots of both schools of positive thinking. The first is that you need to control yourself by overpowering your habitual negativity. The second is that the objective truth about current reality is somehow dangerous to you and that you therefore impose upon the truth a beneficent interpretation.

These assumptions are not a part of the orientation of the creative. The radical difference between positive thinking and the creative orientation can be seen in parallel assumptions about the creative process.

First, in the orientation of the creative, there is no need to control yourself. Instead, the orientation assumes that whether you are habitually negative or not, *you have a natural inclination toward creating what you most truly want.* Furthermore, there are no inner forces to overcome, only inner forces to be aligned organically through vision.

Second, in the orientation of the creative it is essential to report to yourself what current reality truly is, no matter what the conditions and circumstances may be. *A clear description of current reality is necessary input in the creative process.* Were you to impose any "rose-colored" or other synthetic views on your situation, current reality itself would be obscured.

In the orientation of the creative, if you woke up feeling sick, tired, and headachy, you would perceive this as a strategic moment, calling for the Pivotal Technique (see Chapter 12, Strategic Moments): Rather than saying, "I feel great," you would report the truth to yourself, exactly as you observe it. Furthermore, there would be no need to interpret the ultimate meaning of your situation ("Good things always come from these kinds of situations"). Current reality may, of course, include your opinion of the situation, for example, "I feel sick, and I don't like feeling this way."

At this point, in the orientation of the creative you would clarify what you want. You would ask yourself, "How do I want to feel?" or more precisely, "What do I want to create?" You would then report to yourself your answer to the question. You might say, "I want to feel good, energized, vigorous, balanced, and whole." Or you might say, "I want to finish that report at work today." Or you might want something else. Once you had clarified the result you wanted to create you would ask yourself the test question, "If I could have that, would I take it?" You then would give your answer. In doing these two steps you would be clarifying both your current reality and your vision.

The next two steps in the Pivotal Technique are formally to choose the result you want, and then to move on–perhaps get out of bed, perhaps stay in bed, depending on the result you want. Meantime, you allow the structural tension to resolve itself in favor of the result you want. At no moment in the entire process have you used will-power, nor have you felt any need to use it.

TRUTH AND POSITIVE THINKING

What is one major difference between the positive thinking approach and the creative orientation?

In a word, truth.

In the Pivotal Technique in the creative orientation we just used, you will notice that there is no statement which is not factually true. There is no interpretation or denial of the facts. There is only a clear description of what is occurring, and also a clear description of what you want to create. To demonstrate this, let me conduct an imaginary dialogue with you, as if you were the person who used the pivotal technique. I begin by asking:

"Is it true that you woke up this morning feeling badly?"
"Yes."
"Did you report that fact to yourself?"
"Yes."
"Is it true that you don't like feeling badly?"
"Yes."
"Did you add any additional interpretation to your report?"
"No."
"Were you clearly in touch with what you wanted?"
"Yes."
"Did you formally choose what you wanted?"
"Yes."
"So everything you said was true?"
"Yes."

[168]

If I were to conduct a similar dialogue with the person following the first approach to positive thinking, it might go something like this:

"Is it true that you woke up feeling badly this morning?"
"Yes."
"Did you report that feeling to yourself?"
"No."
"What did you do?"
"I said I felt great."
"Was that true?"
"Of course not."
"Therefore, you told a lie."
"Well, I guess I did."

A similar dialogue with the person following the second positive-thinking approach might go like this:

"Is it true that you woke up feeling badly this morning?"
"Yes."
"Did you report that feeling to yourself?"
"Yes."
"Do you like feeling that way?"
"No."
"Did you report your opinion that you don't like feeling that way?"
"No."
"What did you do?"
"I justified feeling badly by asserting it was ultimately beneficial to me."
"Are you in a definitive position to know that that assertion is true? Or is it a supposition or wish on your part? Do you know for sure that feeling badly in this instance is beneficial?"
"Not really. Certainly not directly."
"So rather than simply tell yourself the truth, you tried to impose on yourself an assertion that was designed to control your attitude?"
"Yes."

[169]

In both schools of positive thinking, misrepresentation is involved. In school one, the misrepresentation was an out-and-out lie. In school two, the misrepresentation was to impose an interpretation on events which clouded a true view of those events.

One of the things I like best about the creative orientation is that it is unburdened with gimmicks and fabrications. The orientation of the creative is characterized by forthrightness and honesty. There is never a need to trick yourself or manipulate yourself into any state. There is always a clear choice to move in the direction you want.

Truth and Honesty are nothing like willpower. However, they do release a power–not a power *over* anything, but a power to create what most matters to you, a power to fulfill your human spirit. In the underlying structure of the creative orientation, the path of least resistance leads to where the human spirit is most easily and truthfully expressing itself.

STRONG INTENTION

Nowadays, I often hear people use the word intention in expressions such as, "I have a strong intention to do this or that" or "He has great intentionality." In this context the meaning given to the word "intention" has to do not only with a direction or a leaning toward where you want to go; it has about it also a quality of determination and firmness expressed through will. In one sense intention is simply a more contemporary name for willpower, and one can ask, "How much intention do you need to accomplish something?" Like willpower, intention seems to be measured in quantity. The more intentionality you have, the more effectively you are supposed to be able to produce results–or so the theory goes.

Willpower and intention utilize the same strategy to "deal with" a structural conflict. Recall that in a structural conflict, the path of least resistance leads you first to move in one direction and then to move in the opposite direction, and so on. In such a conflict, the strategy of willpower and intention tries to compensate for the pull toward the belief that you cannot have what you want by attempting to add extra force to the movement toward your desired goal. Like other forms of willpower manipulation, this is an attempt to overpower the structure.

But structure has integrity, and as you try to manipulate the structure by overpowering it, the structure compensates, and the path of least resistance leads you in the opposite direction. Structurally, therefore, *the more intention you use in willpower manipulation, the more intention you will need*, because the intention works against you by increasing the structural pull in the opposite direction.

Carol always saw herself as a person of "great intention." Full of determination and strength, she moved through life with the force of a Mack truck. When she learned to play racquetball, she drove herself to exhaustion. When she worked on a political campaign, she proselytized everyone she knew about her candidate. When her family took a vacation together, she spent most of the time trying to get everyone to have fun. When she prepared to host a dinner party, she compiled lists of every detail of which she could think. During the party, any time there was a small problem such as an ashtray spilling she jumped up and rushed over to clean it up. The effect her "intentionality" had on her guests was that it made them feel tense. Minor problems, normally taken in stride, began to seem enormous to the guests because of the large amount of effort Carol expended on them. At one party, when one of her young children woke up and walked into the middle of the room crying after a bad dream, the way Carol rushed her daughter out of the room only increased everyone's tension.

Carol set out with "great intentions" to accomplish the goal of having a wonderful dinner party, but precisely because of her "great intentions" the dinner party was less successful than she had wanted it to be.

The dinner party was, in microcosm, an example of a willpower manipulation pattern acted out on many stages in Carol's life. When beginning a project, she would plan and prepare in great detail; when anything went wrong, she saw it as a barrier to overcome. She would then increase her intentionality and attempt to overcome what had gone wrong. As she did that, more and more things would go wrong and demand her attention–and intention. In the end, she was always dissatisfied with the outcome. She concluded that she was inadequate and that she needed even stronger intention in the future.

Based on Carol's structural conflict, her strategy of great intention was designed to push her toward a successful dinner party, which was the goal she wanted. The more she planned for it, the more burdened she felt and the harder it was to give the party. The more difficult things seemed, the more she needed to control what might happen at the party. The more Carol pushed toward making the party a success, the more the structure pushed in the opposite direction. In the end, the most probable outcome was for the party to be less successful than she wanted. The more intention she generated, the more the tendency was for the party not to be to her liking.

INTENTION AND CONTROL

Another characteristic of people who express strong intention is their need to control circumstances. Such control is designed to hold things together, so that things do not fall apart. In Carol's case, rushing to clean up the overturned ashtray and ushering her crying daughter out of the room were some of her attempts to hold the dinner party together.

In the creative process, there are times when things fall apart—organically. This occurs when the path of least resistance leads to the disintegration of old forms and the spontaneous formation of new ones. Strongly intentioned people are often insensitive to shifts and changes in the organic process. They attempt to impose their control on the natural play of forces. A dropped ashtray or a crying child may actually enhance a dinner party. Because Carol was so intent on holding the party together, she was unable to appreciate those moments when the form of the party she had preestablished fell apart. She was unaware that such moments could have actually contributed to the kind of party she wanted.

INTENTION AND PROCESS

Another disadvantage in using strong intention is that you tend to focus on process rather than on result. Often, in the name of the result, you may display great willpower. But such willpower is focused almost exclusively on controlling the process which you intend to use to reach your goal.

People of strong intention often commit themselves to a process with great zeal. People commit themselves to psychotherapeutic processes, dietary processes, growth processes, communication processes, business processes, health processes, meditative processes, etc. They become so wedded to a particular process–for releasing emotional stress, for losing weight, for solving problems, for resolving interpersonal problems, for exploring repressed areas of consciousness, for housebreaking their pets–that even if they knew the process was inadequate or noticed that it was no longer working well they would tend to faithfully stay with it.

In the orientation of the creative, it is never wise to marry any process, for *process must serve the result*. The processes which are most useful are the ones which best serve the result. The moment you find a better process to create what you want, use it. At times this might mean recognizing that some of your favorite theories and pet ideas about certain processes are no longer valid. If you have an investment in holding on to those obsolete ways of doing things, you tie your hands before you can even begin creating what you want.

The investments some people have in certain processes are quite extensive. You may have spent thousands of dollars taking various workshops and you may have recommended them to all your friends. You may have written several books on a subject and be publicly known as a champion of some process or other. You may have a lucrative psychotherapeutic or consultant practice in which you have recommended certain processes to your clients. Because of a high investment in certain processes, people often find it difficult to recognize more useful processes when they appear, and are reluctant to use them.

In the orientation of the creative you may find yourself changing direction spontaneously, discovering or gravitating toward new processes which are more useful, and always being open to the possibility that there is a way of getting where you want to go more directly than you had thought.

One characteristic of people in the creative orientation which sometimes puzzles others is how quickly creatively-oriented people can alter the way they have been doing things. In the world of fine arts, it is common for artists to change styles radically–to change from abstract expressionism to photorealism, change media from painting in oils to using acrylics or watercolor, change forms from painting to sculpture, even change aesthetic ideals from Dionysian to Apollonian.

During one of Ghandi's great marches to the sea, thousands of people joined him. Somewhere along the way Ghandi decided to give up the march. His assistants encouraged him to continue, reminding him that many people had left their homes and jobs and were enduring great hardship to be with him. The assistants implied that he had a commitment to these people, and ought to remain consistent in doing what he set out to do. Ghandi's reply was, "My commitment is to the truth as I see it each and every day, not to consistency!"

If you are committed to consistency, it will be difficult for you to be flexible enough to make changes when they are needed. This kind of flexibility can happen only when you are open to whatever natural and organic processes will lead you to the result you want– when you have little investment in a preconceived method of how to get there.

The beauty of the creative orientation lies in its organic quality, its naturalness. In that orientation, you will tend to gravitate to those processes which most effectively contribute to creating the results you want and also express and enhance your true nature. As you create, you naturally evoke that which is highest in you.

CHAPTER 20

ABILITY AND DISCIPLINE

ABILITY AND ENERGY

Moshe Feldenkrais, world-renowned expert on human movement and energy, has said that people of great willpower are often people of very little ability. His observation is astute and accurate. Ability is entirely different from willpower.

Developing willpower, or attempting to increase your inner determination and self-control, is primarily a psychological approach. The use of willpower presumes that there is some inner or outer circumstance needing to be overcome. The energy of willpower is employed not in learning how to create, but in cutting through the "problem." It presupposes that you can effect change primarily through sheer determination, and that the best way to deal with unwelcome circumstances is through self-manipulation. Furthermore, using willpower is an attempt to suppress negative emotions and replace them with feelings and attitudes of confidence, success, and a desire to "do it."

Ability, on the other hand, is not psychological in nature. Developing ability presupposes no particular attitudes or emotions. When you are developing abilities, some days you may feel that you can do nothing wrong and that you are among the smartest persons on the planet, while on other days your attitude may be that you can do nothing right and are among the dumbest on the planet. Some days you may feel inspired, excited, intrigued, entertained, interested, and powerful. Other days you may feel bored, dull, hopeless, indifferent, apathetic, mundane, and powerless. Independent of those experiences, whether positive or negative, you can be developing any ability–learning how to draw, to cook, to type, to speak a foreign language, to ski, to ride horseback, to climb mountains, to solve differential equations, to design computers, to run a meeting, to manage a store, to keep a ledger of accounts.

Ability is developmental. Abilities can grow. In learning to drive a car, you can have more ability tomorrow than you have today. And the more ability you have to drive, the less energy you need to exert when you drive.

As you develop any ability you need to expend less and less energy, and as you increase your facility in using any ability you begin to master the use of your own energy in creating what you want. As you develop willpower, however, you need to expend more and more energy when you use it. As you increase your use of willpower in your life, you begin to feel increasingly powerless. For when you exert willpower in trying to create anything, attempting to control both yourself and the situation, you minimize your capacity to make the subtle adjustments and shifts needed in the creative process.

WILLPOWER VERSUS ABILITY IN TENNIS

Soon after Scott moved into the neighborhood, George invited him to play tennis. George fancied himself to be a good player. He loved tennis, and would play whenever he could. Having Scott around and interested in playing tennis meant he could play more often. Although Scott had played tennis during high school, he had not touched a racquet since then.

During their first match George exerted incredible energy. So did Scott. But George beat his new neighbor soundly in both sets, 6–2, 6–1.

The next time they played George again used tremendous energy against Scott. But this time Scott did not try to keep up with George the way he had during their first match. Instead, he spent the game practicing his returns. He especially began working on his swing, so that he could strategically place the ball where he wanted it to go. But he lost, 6–0, 6–0.

After that, Scott spent an afternoon alone at the court, practicing his serves. He also practiced hitting the ball to specific areas of the court. He was not very good at first. When he attempted to use a stronger swing, the ball mostly hit the net or overshot the foul line. But as he practiced, he was learning. Because he wanted to learn, every miss he made was useful, for from it he was able to learn how to adjust his swing. If he overshot, he tried changing the angle of his racquet or the amount of force he used to hit the ball.

The next time the two men came to the court, George reminded Scott of his poor showing during their last match. George again attempted to trounce Scott, but Scott played better than he had ever played. George beat Scott, 6–3, 6–3.

George and Scott played regularly for the next several weeks, and Scott continued to practice on his own.

After about six weeks, Scott was regularly winning as often as George. George began to hype himself up for each tennis game by giving himself a pep talk, encouraging himself to play harder and exert more effort, telling himself that he could do it. "I can beat this guy," he would say to himself.

After three months, Scott was winning most of the time. In a typical game, George expended enormous amounts of energy as he tried to overpower Scott. George believed that tennis, like many things in life, was something in which you had to "give it your all." He was a noted overachiever. He would throw himself into the game— or whatever he did—with all his energies, in order to succeed. He believed in his own strength of will, and that through his own energy and determination he could prevail. But he was not winning at tennis. No matter how hard he exerted himself, his game did not improve.

Scott, on the other hand, believed that he could develop the abilities he needed to accomplish most things to which he set his mind. He used situations primarily as times to practice learning the abilities he needed. When George played, he only wanted to win. When Scott played, he wanted to master his ability to play tennis.

During the last few months that George and Scott played tennis together, George would exert more energy and determination than he had ever used. He often found himself lunging across the court to make a return, because by this time Scott had developed the ability to place his shots effortlessly in those places least convenient for George to get at them. During a game, George would run back and forth all over the court attempting to return the ball. Since George had all he could do to get the ball back over the net, he could never return it strategically, but only hit it straight to Scott. Thus, Scott was able to stay centered in the court.

At the end of a typical game now, George would walk off the court panting and exhausted, perspiring profusely. Scott would be relaxed, energized, and enthusiastic.

GETTING MAXIMUM RESULTS

George had no chance of improving his game through the exercise of his will. The more willpower he used, the more depleted he became, particularly in the face of Scott's growing ability. Because Scott was focused on mastering his ability to play tennis, he kept improving. It did not matter to him whether or not he won any particular game. In fact, there were many occasions when he was quite willing to lose a game, because he was focused on developing a specific skill.

If you attempt to create the life you want through willpower, you do not learn the abilities you may need to learn along the way. Instead, you expend enormous amounts of energy needlessly and you become insensitive to current reality. Even though George noticed that Scott was winning games, he failed to notice that while Scott was slowly and surely developing the ability to play tennis well, he was not.

If you are developing your ability to create the life you want, you are always in a position of learning those things that would be most helpful to learn. Instead of wastefully depleting your energy as George did, you will be like Scott, using the right amount of energy to develop the abilities you need to give you maximum results.

As you are developing your abilities, current reality provides useful feedback in recognizing how and when to make the necessary adjustments in order to assimilate whatever you have learned.

CREATE AND ADJUST

In developing your ability to create the life you want, there is an important principle to know. It may be stated: *create and adjust*.

In the creative cycle, as all great artists and scientists know, the result you first produce may not match your original vision, and in order to achieve the result you really want you will have to create and adjust. In other words, you first create something, then fix it, to make it better. In the orientation of the creative, no one expects that what you first create will be the final result.

There is a mistaken assumption among some people that great artists and composers create perfectly the first time. The idea seems to be that artists have an inspiration, then simply execute the work of art as if germination were followed instantly by creation.

In studying Beethoven's work, Roger Sessions shows how Beethoven would create and adjust, perhaps many times, even in writing his greatest music.

> I have in my possession the last movement of his "Mannerklavier Sonata"; the sketches show him carefully modeling, then testing in systematic and apparently cold-blooded fashion, the theme of the fugue. Where, one might ask, is the inspiration here? Yet if the word has any meaning at all, it is certainly appropriate to this movement, with its irresistible and titanic energy of expression, already present in the theme.

Beethoven's inspirational vision was not lost with his "modeling, then testing," rather it arose, as Sessions wisely points out, "from the original inspiration, and is, so to speak, an extension of its logic."

D. H. Lawrence described the process of creating and adjusting a painting.

> In a couple of hours there it all was, man, woman, child, blue shirt, red shirt, red shawl, pale room–all in the rough, but, as far as I am concerned, a picture. The struggling comes later. But the picture itself comes in the first rush, or not at all. It is only when the picture has come into being that one can struggle and make it *grow* to completion.

What you create in your life at first is like a first draft of a picture you want to paint. The next step is to adjust that first draft to bring it more in line with your vision.

Continue to make adjustments until you have created something that satisfies your vision. As you make each adjustment you are learning, as have all the great artists and composers, specifically about what it is you are creating, and generally about your individual and unique creative process. Each adjustment you make strengthens your ability to create, even when the adjustment itself does not seem to work. Because Scott was focused on mastering tennis, even the serves he misplaced, the returns he failed to make, and the games he lost helped strengthen his ability to play tennis and to become the kind of tennis player he wanted to be.

NASA MASTERS SPACE

The history of the United States Space Program is filled with examples of the "create and adjust" principle. From the earliest days of the program, every rocket that was launched was part of an attempt to master rocketry. Beginning with the first manned space flight of Alan Shepard, each astronaut contributed to the accumulated knowledge and experience, which was then handed on to the next group of astronauts to travel in space.

In the early days of NASA (the United States' National Aeronautics and Space Administration), many experiments failed. Rockets blew up on the launching pad, or shortly after launch. Guidance systems malfunctioned and rockets had to be destroyed by ground control. Aerospace engineers examined varieties of fuel systems, guidance systems, navigational systems, tracking systems, ground-to-capsule communication systems, and on-board computer systems. They adopted some and rejected others. Some that they adopted had later to be adjusted. Each mistake contributed as much as each success to NASA's ability.

The Space Program gained new power in the early 1960's with the clear vision President John F. Kennedy gave it, "to land a man on the moon and safely return him to earth by the end of the decade."

Once that vision was in place, an incredible burst of creative technological advancement occurred in the United States. Engineers and technicians had a clear focus for their energy: get a man to the moon and back. With that focus, they were able to make the kinds of adjustments needed to make this vision a reality, creating new concepts and even new fields of science, rejecting certain time-honored engineering principles, inventing new materials, new lubricants, and new alloys that would withstand rapid changes in temperature from the cold of absolute zero to more than 2000 degree heat.

It may have taken Kennedy five minutes or less to formulate in words the vision of a man landing on the moon and safely returning to earth within the decade. But it took NASA scientists eight years to create and adjust enough to develop the technical abilities to fulfill that vision.

Throughout the 1970's, with unmanned exploratory probes to other planets and beyond, and throughout the 1980's, with development of the space shuttle and networks of communication satellites, the technological advances continue.

The story of NASA's progress in creating the Space Program could be symbolized by the image of a single rocket making its way to the moon. For even though the rocket successfully reaches the moon it will, in fact, be off course more than 90 percent of the time. Since any rocket tends to fly off in a straight-line tangent, continual navigational adjustments have to be made to keep it on course. Only with such continual adjustments can it arrive at its final destination.

Once you have envisioned the final destination, or the result you want to create, making adjustments becomes a major activity in the creative process.

Vincent Van Gogh thoroughly understood this principle:

> The thing has already taken form in my mind before I start on it. The first attempts are absolutely unbearable. I say this because I want you to know that if you see something worthwhile in what I am doing, it is not by accident but because of real direction and purpose.

As you assimilate each new adjustment, you are organically developing pertinent abilities. The reason formulas and conventions do not usually live up to their promise to produce the results you want is that they usually preclude developing and assimilating new and possibly necessary abilities along the way.

Developing abilities with every new creation is, first and foremost, a learning experience. It is also almost exclusively experimental. *In the creative process, to a greater or lesser degree, all actions are experiments.*

Van Gogh experimented with different vantage points of perspective in the same painting as well as with light, color, texture, patterns, composition, subject matter, and expression. This led to his extraordinary originality and the mastery of his own unique artistic style. Such experimentation is not reserved only for the fine arts.

Scott was continuously experimenting in his approach to playing tennis. He learned from those experiments, and was able to put that learning into practice in subsequent experiments. Each time he experimented, he assimilated what he learned, thereby increasing his overall ability—not only his ability to play tennis but, even more than that, his ability to increase all of his abilities.

DISCIPLINE AND ABILITY

The word "discipline" evokes terror in the hearts of many people. It may conjure up a variety of images—a grammar school student attempting to memorize the multiplication table or a long poem, runners getting up at five o'clock every morning for months to build endurance for a marathon, children being forced to practice the piano for years, members of a parade-marching team drilling in close formation for hours, recruits in rigorous training at military boot camp, obedient monks in a monastery following a strict regimen.

In the reactive-responsive orientation, discipline is most often viewed as a negative experience—one in which you force yourself to do something unpleasant and difficult, though ultimately for your own good. This is sometimes called "self-discipline."

Discipline is also often seen as imposed from outside. Such discipline happens when you are forced by someone else to do something against your will. Parents and teachers usually discipline children. In some schools, the word discipline means punishment. There, a student who is considered a discipline problem is told, "Report after school for 'discipline'."

DISCIPLINE AND CONFLICT MANIPULATION

In the reactive-responsive orientation self-discipline is often used as a strategy to deal with some form of structural conflict. You may use it as a strategy designed to overcome your lack of ability. George used willpower in an attempt to overcome his lack of ability in tennis. But he could also have used self-discipline by forcing himself to practice in order to improve his game. He would have had to force himself because he did not want to practice, he simply wanted to win. George would define self-discipline as forcing or self-manipulating yourself, for your own good, into doing something you do not want to do.

DISCIPLINE AND SECONDARY CHOICE

In the orientation of the creative, discipline and self-discipline mean something completely different. They never involve coercing or manipulating yourself into taking action you really do not want to take. When you are in the creative orientation, you actually always do what you want. Secondary choice is the key to understanding discipline. *In the creative orientation, using self-discipline means making effective secondary choices.*

Once you know what your primary choice is, making secondary choices which support that primary choice becomes natural. Once Scott made the primary choice to master tennis-playing, his secondary choices to practice his swing and his serve during free time as well as his secondary choice to use the games with George primarily as times for developing his ability were natural choices for him to make.

When I say that in the creative orientation you always do what you want, this does not mean that you simply follow the whims of your changing moods, and that when you don't feel like studying or practicing, you don't. What I mean is that, because the result you want is always clear to you, it enables you to generate whatever actions you need to take in order to complete the secondary choices you make.

When you are in the orientation of the creative discipline is not a conflict-manipulation strategy, but rather the art of making secondary choices which aid in creating what you want. When structural tension is created it spontaneously generates energy, which may be directly applied in carrying out your secondary choices. Making these secondary choices becomes easier than not making them because they lie along the path of least resistance.

CREATING STRUCTURAL TENSION ANEW

The power that enables you to make secondary choices easily comes from structural tension. However, *structural tension must be regularly created anew.* One of the most common mistakes I have seen people in the creative orientation make is thinking that they are creating structural tension when they are not.

David had a vision of getting a Master's degree in Business Administration from Stanford University. When he first formulated the result he wanted his current reality included a regular nine-to-five job in a company he liked; he also had tremendous enthusiasm for going to graduate school, and it was likely that he would be easily able to balance his graduate work with his job and family.

Three months into the semester, David seemed to have run out of steam. He found it increasingly difficult to complete his research assignments at school, and he was having trouble balancing his life at home and at work.

David kept remembering how strongly he had wanted the MBA degree, and he kept remembering the well-balanced current reality he had when he first enrolled at the university. And yet, structural tension did not seem to be working for him, for he had less and less energy to make certain necessary secondary choices.

One day on his way to class, David began to wonder if he actually wanted his degree. Normally, in situations like this in the past, he would have concluded that he no longer wanted what he had originally set out for. But this time it occurred to him to do the Pivotal Technique as a way of creating new structural tension.

As a first step he asked himself what current reality was for him. He realized that current reality was no longer what it originally had been three months before, when his life was well-balanced, he was full of enthusiasm for his new graduate program, and his job and family life were running smoothly. That was the last time he had formally made a point of noticing current reality. So he spent three or four minutes observing his present current reality. He described to himself the situation in which he now found himself, which included: finding it difficult to complete research assignments at school, struggling with studies, and feeling more and more demands being placed on him by his family and job.

As a second step, he asked himself, "Do I really want an MBA degree from Stanford?" He separated what he wanted from what he thought possible, and so he considered the question independently of his disappointing experiences during recent weeks. He asked himself, "If I could have the MBA degree, would I take it?" He realized he actually did still care very much about having that degree. He answered "yes."

As the final steps in the Pivotal Technique, he formally made the choice to have the MBA degree, and then went back to what he was doing before he began the technique, namely, walking to class.

For the next three weeks, David had renewed enthusiasm for his graduate work, and within two days after doing the Pivotal Technique his job and his family life again seemed to be in balance.

After three weeks, however, David was feeling disappointed as he noticed that he was experiencing the same kinds of difficulties he had experienced before he did the technique. So he did the technique again, and again within two days he was back on track, and so was everything else in his life.

The next time, at the moment he began to get that familiar disappointed feeling, he quickly did the Pivotal Technique. It seemed to take effect immediately. From that time on David stayed in touch with what he wanted (his vision) and with what current reality was. He made a point of observing current reality regularly, as well as of finding out if he still wanted what he had originally wanted.

Rather than losing energy and momentum as he had in the past, he began to be more excited and enthusiastic about his work, his family, and his graduate studies. He was easily able to make the secondary choices necessary to complete his degree successfully, and he graduated near the top of his class.

KEEPING STRUCTURAL TENSION STRONG

When David was not really in touch with his vision and an up-to-date version of his current reality, structural tension was weakened. As he lost touch with what he wanted, he shifted from the orientation of the creative back to the reactive-responsive orientation, where he began to try to force himself into doing his assignments. In that context, the path of least resistance led to more difficulty, including problems at home and at work.

When he re-examined what result he wanted to create (vision) and observed where he presently was (current reality), structural tension was created anew, and his orientation shifted back to the creative. The discrepancy between his current reality and his vision spontaneously gave rise to energy, which enabled him to fulfill easily all of the necessary choices connected to his vision.

When you are in touch with what you want and in touch with current reality, the underlying structure leads you directly to the result you want. However, when you are only remembering what it was you once wanted, or remembering how current reality used to be the last time you looked, structural tension is weakened or lost.

Creation is ongoing. For your vision to be alive, it must be alive *now*. In a sense, it must be "current vision." Although most often the vision of the result you want to create does not radically change, occasionally it does. One of your functions during a creative cycle is to continue to create a fresh view of your vision as well as a fresh view of your current reality. In working with structural tension, do this regularly.

With practice, you will assimilate the ability to create structural tension as a general ability. Creating structural tension will become automatic as you habitually look at where you are and where you want to be. It will become a part of your normal state of being.

CHAPTER 21

CREATING WHAT MATTERS

THE PERFECT RELATIONSHIP

Many people want a deeply satisfying love relationship. When you are in the reactive-responsive orientation, wanting such a love relationship often has little to do with the other person. Instead, it primarily has to do with what that relationship is supposed to provide you in the way of personal fulfillment–security, companionship, being "saved," etc. It is not sought for its own sake, as it would be if you simply loved someone and wanted to be with them, but for the "needs" it can satisfy in your life.

In the reactive-responsive orientation, real human relationships are next to impossible to create, because reactive-responsive people usually impose unspoken demands on the people with whom they relate.

When I ask people in the reactive-responsive orientation, "What do you want in a relationship?" followed by, "And what will that do for you?", I often hear a list of requirements which the people say their partners must provide for them. Their requirements usually include:

"My partner must nurture me . . . love me unconditionally . . . be supportive . . . give me enough room . . . never be critical . . . be interested in what I have to say . . . leave me alone when I want to be left alone . . . not be demanding . . . be open and understanding . . . provide me with sexual satisfaction . . . encourage my personal and spiritual growth . . . bring out the best in me . . . inspire me . . . have a great sense of humor . . . be entertaining . . . make me happy . . . etc., etc."

When reactive-responsive people who want a relationship go to a party, what they commonly do is survey the guests, looking for likely prospects to fulfill their list of requirements. They measure each guest against their standards of how a person should be in order for them to have a relationship with that person.

To reactive-responsive people, other individuals are seen not as separate human beings with personality, character, and aspirations unique unto themselves, but rather as candidates for a "position" the reactive-responsive person is seeking to fill. For reactive-responsive people, the ultimate value of these candidates stems from the potential they may have to alter the circumstances of the reactive-responsive person's life in ways that would bring fulfillment and happiness.

THE BURDEN OF FULFILLMENT

When one reactive-responsive person finds another reactive-responsive person to relate to, they usually impose on each other the burden of providing fulfillment and happiness. They do not see each other as authentic human beings, but rather as need-fulfillment machines. They assign to each other the job of fulfilling whatever needs they may generate. Occasionally, at the beginning of their relationship, they do experience some degree of satisfaction. But usually this is soon followed by disappointment and disillusionment.

Reactive-responsive people often talk about how their relationship is "going." If their needs are being fulfilled, they say that their relationship is going well. If their needs are not being met by their partner, they say that the relationship is not going well.

If you are thinking, "Why else would one be in a relationship except to fulfill one's needs?" you are probably in a reactive-responsive orientation in your relationships. The beauty, power, and specialness of real relationships has most likely never been yours. Reactive-responsive people often accept a shallow substitute for what could be most profound and meaningful in life.

When you place others in the position of being in charge of your personal fulfillment, you miss experiencing who they really are, and the reality of your *real* relationship with them is obscured.

In putting other people in charge of creating your happiness, you assign to them a responsibility which is not theirs at all, but yours. For no one but you is in charge of what you create in life.

When you put your power outside yourself, you reinforce your experience of powerlessness. In such a case, the path of least resistance for any relationship you have will always lead to disappointment, dissatisfaction, and a situation in which you are less and less able to be yourself.

TOOTHPASTE AND ROMANCE

In our society much emphasis is placed on romantic love, as if romantic love were the ultimate source of personal fulfillment and salvation.

Some toothpaste commercials on television promise that if you use their toothpaste you will be blessed with a romantic, fulfilling, sexy, gorgeous partner.

Such a toothpaste commercial provides a strikingly clear portrayal of the reactive-responsive orientation. First, its underlying assumption is that the power in your life resides outside of you in the circumstances, in this case, in the brand of toothpaste you use. Second, this assumption is reinforced by the proposition that if you use the right toothpaste, your current circumstances will change in such a way as to provide you with romance. Third, it is assumed in the commercial that this romance will bring you happiness and save you from unhappiness. In a more general form, the three-step sequence is: the right response begets a change of circumstances in your life, and the change of circumstances begets a desired effect. In this case, toothpaste begets romance, and romance begets happiness.

WHAT YOU CREATE

In the reactive-responsive orientation the "desired effect" being sought is almost always burdened with ulterior motives. Thus results are desired not for their own sake, but for some purpose or effect ultimately relating to self-enhancement.

In the orientation of the creative, however, there is a major difference in the relationship you have with the results you want to create. Primarily these results are something you want to see exist, independent of any meaning or motive related to self-enhancement. Very much as Leonardo da Vinci painted "The Last Supper" so that the painting could exist as an individual entity separate from his life, you as creator bring forth creations which are individual entities. What you create has a life of its own. Why you create it is to give it life. Like parents bringing forth children, you are both father and mother of that which you create.

The creative orientation is touched by irony, for you are both champion and critic of what you create; you are passionate toward it (you love it enough to bring it into existence) yet dispassionate (your identity is not tied to the identity of what you create, and you are ready to change or even destroy it at any moment if doing so will further the realization of your vision). The American composer Alan Hovanness at a certain point in his development once destroyed an entire body of his music–representing years of work–in order to build a unique individual and personal style of music he had envisioned. What you create is both a part of you and separate from you.

EXPRESSING YOUR VALUES

In the reactive-responsive orientation, the highest values expressed revolve around survival, security, and salvation (the ultimate resolution of all conflict).

In the orientation of the creative, the highest human values revolve around choice, creation, human aspiration, spiritual aspiration, and spiritual purpose.

In the reactive-responsive orientation, since survival is a major goal in life, people look to formula and convention in hopes of assuring their survival; aspiration must be kept limited to that which is known and safe; and the individual is reduced to being self-serving, opportunistic, and self-absorbed.

The way you live your life expresses your values. If you primarily live a reactive-responsive life, the values you are expressing are about protecting yourself from harm, avoiding emotional discomfort, and resolving conflict. You may even pursue comfort and the reduction of conflict in the name of higher values, as when people pursue spirituality not primarily to do God's work but so that they can be "saved."

If you live the life-orientation of the creative, among the values you are expressing are truth, freedom, justice, and commitment to that which is truly highest in you.

YOUR HIGHER PURPOSE

When you live in the orientation of the creative, there is another value which expresses itself through your actions and aspirations. It is the value which may be described as fulfilling the unique higher purpose of your life, the meaning that your life has in this moment in human history.

In the orientation of the creative there is an implicit recognition that you represent the realization of possibilities for humanity beyond the individual circumstances of your life, that you have contained within your being–perhaps independently of the way you have lived your life up to this point–a certain true greatness, a greatness which transcends what you yourself may be able to recognize. And yet you know it is there, for the depths of your being long for it.

THE PRECIOUSNESS OF THE MOMENT

In the reactive-responsive orientation people often make things matter that really don't matter–for example, looking good, seeking approval, impressing others, accumulating symbols of worth such as money or prestige, nursing grievances, getting revenge, proving somebody wrong so that they be seen as "right," and so on. Much of their time, energy, and focus are directed toward values they themselves do not care about.

In the orientation of the creative, you make matter what really matters to you, so that your time, energy, and focus are directed toward values you care about.

Because a major strategy of the reactive-responsive orientation is to avoid the full recognition of current reality, a certain numbness or unconsciousness often prevails. The beauty and potential of current reality are missed.

One important aspect of current reality is that *everything is temporary*. Anything which has a beginning will eventually have an end. Your life on this planet had a beginning and eventually will have an end. The lives of the people you love, the people to whom you are indifferent, and the people you dislike will also have an end. All of the circumstances in which you find yourself will sooner or later come to an end. Even the life of this planet itself will eventually end. Current reality includes mortality. Mortality defines life as precious and unique.

Many people who have had near-death or death experiences and continued to live have changed. They have often entirely rearranged their values, becoming acutely aware that they live in a temporal frame and that each moment has a meaning, purpose, possibility, and existence all its own.

Years ago I taught music composition at The New England Conservatory. Often in my classes, in order to demonstrate certain compositional techniques, I would spontaneously compose exquisite little pieces on the chalkboard. After each class was over, I would erase the new compositions without ever writing them down to save them. The moments in those classes were often magical and precious, for the music that was created there had never existed before and was never to exist again. Being a part of the class meant that you were in the presence of something special and unique. Being in the class was a poignant time which re-defined the nature of all the other moments in life, whether they were short moments (minutes, hours, days) or long moments (months, years, lifetimes).

In the 1960's, there was a great visionary jazz musician named Eric Dolphy, whose very last recording was titled "Last Date." Just after this recording was made, he died tragically in an automobile accident. At the end of the recording he said prophetically, "Music, when it's in the air, is gone . . . You can never get it back . . . It's gone."

Eric Dolphy understood the preciousness of the moment. In improvisational jazz, perhaps more than in any other musical genre, there is an appreciation of spontaneity and an understanding of the temporary nature of both art and life. Even jazz which is recorded, as Eric Dolphy knew so well, is heard in a continually changing reality, so that the same recording is not really the same music each time it is played.

In the orientation of the creative spontaneity is possible because current reality is ever-changing, shaping and reshaping itself, coming together and falling apart. It is always new, whether familiar or unfamiliar. Spontaneity is possible when you become aware that current reality is always new and unique, when you realize that each new moment provides fresh possibilities, is alive, is one-of-a-kind.

People in the reactive-responsive orientation rarely have any awareness that each moment is new and different. In fact, because of the underlying structure in play in that orientation most moments seem similar, if not identical to other moments. Reactive-responsive people play out the same patterns over and over again. This is because, as we have seen, the path of least resistance inherent in the underlying structure always leads them through the same sequence.

WHAT YOU VALUE

What you value–what matters most to you, what you hold dear, what you reach for, what you make important–is one of the major factors which enables a shift from the orientation of the reactive-responsive to the orientation of the creative.

If you try to change your values in order to change your orientation, however, it will not work–for three reasons. First of all, changing your values is a gesture of the reactive-responsive orientation, for you are treating your values as if they were circumstantial stimuli, hoping that if you alter them perhaps your condition will change. Second, such a change would be an attempt to impose one value system over another, with little regard for whether or not the new values are in fact truly your values. Third, by this gesture you are likely to be continuing to express your original values (survival, self-enhancement, etc.) in the name of the new values of truth, freedom, justice, and so on.

If you attempt to change your values in order to change your circumstances and it is unclear whether the new values are really yours, you are assuming that by giving the right response (changing your values), circumstances will be changed and the new circumstances will in turn change your life. This is not unlike the sequence of steps by which toothpaste is supposed to beget romance, and romance, in turn, happiness.

Unfortunately, attempting to get people to change their values (or imposing values on people when they do not change them willingly) is a common failing. This attempt is often found in religions and approaches to "developing human potential." In these contexts, the toothpaste-begets-romance-begets-happiness formula is usually translated into: new values beget new circumstances, and these circumstances beget happiness; i.e., spiritual or holistic fulfillment.

When values are imposed on you, either by yourself or others, this imposition provides no real foundation for any lasting change, because the underlying structure has as its path of least resistance eventual movement away from the new values and back to the familiar old ones.

Every year millions of people adopt new values when they begin new spiritual practices or apply new techniques of psychology and human potential. Such people often revert back to their original values in a relatively short time, because the adoption of the new values was primarily motivated by the reactive-responsive orientation.

It is truly astonishing to see to what degree people pursue higher goals starting from values which are primarily concerned with self. It is not that such people are not well-intentioned, but rather that their level of awareness of themselves is very limited.

REALIZING YOUR TRUE VALUES

Certain religions and approaches to human potential play into the reactive-responsive structure by attempting to impose on individuals that which is supposed to be in their best interests.

But in the end the real questions every individual must face are: What is the truth? What is my real nature? What are my values? What do I truly care about?

Most people do not actually know their answers to these questions because they have not looked, explored, considered what matters most to them and what their life is about.

Only by genuine "soul-searching" can you know where you stand. Merely guessing, assuming or hoping that your values are clear, far from helping to create the underlying structure of the creative orientation, reinforces the structure of the reactive-responsive orientation.

There is no substitute for knowing what truly matters to you. No one else can tell you the answer, "so then you'll know." You cannot even tell yourself what ought to truly matter to you, in an attempt to impose those values on yourself. The only foundation for the creative orientation that you can have is one built on truth–the truth about your nature.

Many people believe that their nature is essentially evil, negative, and destructive, and that somehow they need to overcome this evil nature in order to keep it in check. But they miss the obvious. For who but a good person would attempt to make sure that destructive and negative tendencies did not manifest themselves?

As I said earlier, what you value is one of the major factors that enables you to shift from the reactive-responsive orientation to the orientation of the creative. It is not the imposition of a new value system I am talking about here, but *a shift to the realization of your true values*.

Often people who have freedom, truth, justice and love as their truly highest values obscure that fact by attempting to *impose* these very same values on themselves. If by your very nature you are good and then attempt to impose goodness on yourself, you imply that your very nature is other than good. (Why else would you need to impose goodness on yourself?)

The questions that are always important to ask yourself are: What is the truth? What is really going on? And not: what should the truth be? And how can I impose it on myself?

THE POWER TO CREATE

Over and over again I have seen people, when reunited with their power to create, aspire to what is highest in humanity: freedom, justice, peace, love, purpose, truth. No one tells them that these are the values to which they should aspire. These values emanate from what they truly care about.

Once you know yourself on that level, you begin to build the new structure of the creative orientation, in which reality is not a threat but a welcome experience and vision is not pie in the sky but the concrete expression of what most matters to you.

In a conversation with friends, the Apollo astronaut Rusty Schweikert was asked, "What was it really like in outer space?"

He grew silent and then said, "You're in space . . . and you look down upon the earth . . . and it's so beautiful . . . it looks like a baby that's about to be born."

In the orientation of the creative, every moment has the kind of potential that Rusty Schweikert described for the planet–something about to be born that has never existed before, may not have even been imagined before, and yet can exist and will exist through an act of your own creation.

You as creator can bring into existence what has never existed before. From nothing you can bring forth that which matters.

CHAPTER 22

THE POWER
OF TRANSCENDENCE

THE DETERMINING FACTOR

Many adults feel they are trapped by their past. They think they are doomed by events that have happened to them in the earliest stages of their childhood.

Some people imagine that the birth experience was so traumatic that it completely determined the course of their life; for them, the biggest problem they have is that they were born.

Some believe that they are victims of their conditioning or how their parents treated them; they see this as the predominant determining factor in the life they now lead.

There are those who propose that they are extensions of their genes and that what primarily determines their life-experiences is their DNA genetic code.

Others assign the ultimate determining factor of their lives to their astrological makeup or to their numerology.

Still others attribute the determining factor of their lives to their social, ethnic, class, and racial background.

Some say it is their gender that mostly determines their fate.

There are many theories, built primarily on the assumptions of the reactive-responsive orientation, which promote the idea that you are for the most part fixed in your life-pattern, and that most changes—if changes are at all possible—must be made by somehow dealing with the determined nature you carry within you. Different theories suggest dealing with the determining factor by understanding it, overpowering it, denying it, manipulating it, experiencing it, accepting it, repressing it, surrendering to it, dialoguing with it, appeasing it, or integrating it.

The reactive-responsive orientation finds this notion of determining factors appealing, because it attributes causality to circumstances beyond your direct control. Furthermore, it implies that by altering your *relationship* to the determining circumstances (that is, by developing new and more sophisticated methods of responding to these determining circumstantial stimuli), you can rid yourself of the oppression that resides within you.

Many people think that once they are able to straighten out their past they will find the solution to their problems, and then they will be free to live the lives they want. But even if they find the "solution" to their "problem," they still need to create the life they want. Merely finding solutions does not *cause* fulfillment and happiness to happen.

The underlying structures in play in a person's life determine the tendencies of thought, action, and movement. And these tendencies will usually be fulfilled, because the path of least resistance leads to their fulfillment.

Instead of attempting to alter the "determining circumstances" or your relationship to them, as is done in the reactive-responsive orientation, you can change the underlying structure of your life, so that the path of least resistance will lead in the direction you want to go.

It is the organic order of nature, and not how you react or respond to the circumstances of your life, which gives rise to the possibility that you can become and be the predominant force in your own life. It is not *against* nature that this shift to the orientation of the creative can happen but *through* nature. One aspect of the creative orientation is that of mastering cause and effect, so that the dominant determining factor is not your past, your genetic code, your astrology, or your diet, but rather *what you choose*.

You might be thinking that the factors that have been prevalent in your life up to this point are so powerful, have created so much momentum, have existed for such a long time, and are so overwhelming, that there is very little you can do because of them. You may have even tried, time and again, to change your life situation by changing yourself, your job, your spouse, your psychology, and your diet, only to find that nothing of real significance has changed and that even in new settings and new relationships you are still entrenched in old familiar life circumstances.

Change is possible. But it can only come when it is rooted in the service of that which you most deeply care about, and not when you are trying to "solve" yourself or your life as if they were "problems."

When you shift to the orientation of the creative you begin to move along the path of mastering causality. You become the predominant causal force in your life, which is a natural and desirable situation.

This shift is made by evoking senior forces such as fundamental choice, primary and secondary choices, structural tension, aspiration to your true values, and being true to yourself. These senior forces always take priority over lesser forces such as willpower manipulation, conflict manipulation, and structural conflict.

There is another force inherent in the orientation of the creative which is senior even to mastering causality. This senior force I call *transcendence*.

TRANSCENDENCE

Transcendence is the power to be born anew, to make a fresh start, to turn over a new leaf, to begin with a clean slate, to enter into a state of grace, to have a second chance.

Transcendence makes no reference to the past, whether your past has been overflowing with victories or filled with defeats. When you enter a state of transcendence you are able to create a new life, unburdened by both the victories and the defeats of the past.

Transcendence is more than just the accurate realization that the past is over. It is also a realignment of all dimensions of yourself with the very source of your life.

The story of Charles Dickens' character Scrooge in *A Christmas Carol* is the epitome of the power of transcendence. Guided by the Christmas Spirits, Scrooge was able to see his past, his present, and his probable future, and he was then given a second chance at life. When Scrooge awoke on Christmas morning, the very fact that he was still alive was the gift that provided new possibilities–including a new way of living which, up to that point in the story, had seemed improbable and even impossible.

Another major character in the story is Tiny Tim, the lame and sickly yet uncommonly wise child who symbolizes natural human goodness. Scrooge developed a special relationship with Tiny Tim during the night with the Spirits. When Scrooge asked the Spirit of Christmas Present whether Tiny Tim would survive the Spirit replied, "If these shadows remain unaltered, I see a vacant chair beside the hearth and a crutch without an owner, carefully preserved."

Scrooge's reaching out to Tiny Tim and Tiny Tim's reaching out to Scrooge were catalysts in Scrooge's transcendence. In fact, by his transcendence, he was able to save Tiny Tim's life just as Tiny Tim was able to save Scrooge's life. Scrooge was able to redeem himself through his relationship to and innate love of the natural human goodness which Tiny Tim symbolized.

When you re-establish your relationship to your natural goodness, what is highest in you is given a new life.

From the moment he awoke on that Christmas morning through the rest of his life, Scrooge was truly changed. The change was not merely a superficial change in behavior. Rather it was a change in his entire life-orientation. Scrooge realized the preciousness of each moment and his ability to aspire to the greatest good in each moment.

Had Scrooge merely had a peak experience, no fundamental change in orientation would have occurred. While a peak experience might have temporarily changed his behavior, in time he would have tended to revert to his old, miserly ways.

Because Scrooge's change was orientational, he was fundamentally a new person, as if he had been born anew. From that point on his past was irrelevant, and the nature of his change filled each subsequent day of his life.

Not all changes of orientation, even desirable ones, contain the power of transcendence. It is possible for you to have a change of orientation and still continue to be in a linear, cause-and-effect system. Transcendence operates outside such a system. Transcendence evokes the power to start from scratch, outside the realm where previous causal actions are in play. Because transcendence is an ever new state of being, once you enter into it each new moment is alive with fresh possibilities–possibilities which may never have seemed possible before.

THE PRODIGAL SON

Another story which exquisitely illustrates the principle of transcendence is the Parable of the Prodigal Son.

In the story there was a father who had two sons. One of his sons left home and went astray, while the other was a "good boy" who stayed at home and worked with his father.

At a certain point in the story the prodigal son remembered his home, and he returned to his father without any expectations of what might happen to him or how he would be received.

When he arrived home, his father, who had thought the boy was dead, was so overjoyed to discover his son alive that he celebrated the homecoming with great festivity. Not only did the father accept the prodigal back with all the rights a full son, but he celebrated his love for his son far more than if the prodigal had never left at all.

The "good" son who had remained at home all these years was outraged at the father's accepting and rejoicing over the prodigal. When the "good" son came to the father to protest what he was doing, the father tried to explain his actions by saying, "You see, I thought he was dead . . . but he's alive." ("I thought he was dead, but he lives.")

The father and his two sons represent three separate and distinct aspects of yourself. The father represents the source of your life, the good son is the part of you that has been aligned to that source, and the prodigal son is the part of you that has become disaligned with your source, the part of you that has gone astray from being true to yourself and true to what is highest in you.

There is a point at which the prodigal, reactive and rebellious part of you *remembers* your source and desires to return to it, as did the prodigal son in the parable.

Furthermore, as in the story, your source longs to be reunited with all of you and reaches out to you as the father reached out to receive the prodigal.

But the "good" part of you–the part of you that has tried through the years to respond appropriately, to be true to yourself, and to do the right things–rejects the reunion of all the parts of yourself. It is not the prodigal aspects of yourself that deny your full integration, but the part of you that has been responsive, the part of you that has tried to be a good person.

Most people assume that it is their prodigal side–their indiscretions, failings, compromises, lies, dishonesty, opportunistic behavior, selfishness, hatreds, prejudices, jealousies, pettiness, greed, egotism, laziness, destructiveness, negativity, and rebelliousness– that keeps them from reuniting with what is highest in them, their source. However, the immediate natural tendency of the prodigal part of yourself is to want to return "home" to your source and be realigned with it.

It is not your prodigal side that prevents you from forgiving yourself, but the "good" part of you. It is the "good," responsive part of you that rejects your innately strong longing to be one with yourself.

When the prodigal son remembered that he could return home, he did so without any expectations–unconditionally.

When you awaken to your deepest longing to be whole, you return to wholeness without making demands, without setting up expectations, without establishing any conditions.

Similarly, as the father rejoiced over the return of his prodigal son, so your source welcomes you home without conditions, tests of sincerity, or expectations of contrition, explanations, or repayment.

This unconditional love that the father (source) has and his great longing for your return is the very power that enables transcendence to occur. "I thought he was dead . . . and I find he's alive."

ONE-WAY BARGAINS

In order to have the return of the prodigal complete and whole, reconciliation between the two sons also needed to happen. However, at this point, there was a twist in the story. In the beginning of the story, the father and the son who stayed at home are aligned, while the prodigal son is disaligned. When the prodigal returned to the father, however, the prodigal and the father were aligned, but the good son became disaligned. How did this change come about?

The good son had made what may be called a "one-way bargain" with the father. In a typically reactive-responsive way he assumed that if he did all of the "right things" and adhered to the "right standards" and followed the "right precepts," he would be rewarded by the father. He was shocked to see his brother who had not followed the "right path" being welcomed, honored, and celebrated.

Many people make similar one-way bargains. The form of this unilateral bargain is for one person to assume that if they follow certain practices, others (or perhaps even the universe itself) must reciprocate in some way. In a one-way bargain the other party never really agrees to the bargain, and often does not even know of it.

A classic example of a one-way bargain is found in the early stages of many relationships when one person unilaterally decides not to date any other people, with the implicit demand that the other person in the relationship do likewise. It is a one-way bargain if the other person never makes that agreement.

There are those who attempt to live "good" lives as a one-way bargain with the universe. They decide that if they are "good," the universe must reciprocate and be good to them. The trouble is, the universe did not make that agreement with them.

In the parable, the good son's actions were part of a one-way bargain, tied to the rewards he expected from his father. But that was not an agreement the father had made with him.

If the good son had been righteous because he wanted to be, rather than for the reward he expected from his father, his actions would have been their own reward. The parable implies, however, that the good son was good for an ulterior motive. In a typically reactive-responsive way, the good son did what he thought he *had* to do, not what he truly wanted to do.

The part of you that has created one-way bargains with yourself is like the good son. If you find it difficult to forgive yourself for not having been true to yourself in the past, one reason might be because you have made such a bargain.

BEING PERFECT

Many people demand perfection of themselves and others. But we exist on an imperfect plane of reality in which, ironically, the only perfection that can be found is in its imperfection.

Viktor Frankl points out in *Man's Search for Meaning* that the saints did not reach sainthood by trying to be perfect. Many of the people I see in workshops begin with the notion that they have to be perfect. They then blame themselves for being imperfect, and refuse to forgive themselves for their many "transgressions."

No one can forgive you but yourself–including forgiving the "good" part of you that has sought perfection and made it hard to forgive yourself until now. But when you come home to yourself without expectations, demands, ulterior motives, or one-way bargains, a fundamental change in the underlying structure of your life takes place. And its path of least resistance now leads you into a state of transcendence, in which total integration of your life cannot help but occur.

While the goal of responsiveness in the reactive-responsive orientation is an impossible-to-reach perfection, the natural tendency in the orientation of the creative is transcendence.

THE POWER OF THE SOURCE/THE POWER OF THE PRIMAL SELF

What enables transcendence to supercede the power of cause and effect is that in the structural play of forces transcendence is a senior force and, like all senior forces, takes priority over lower forces.

Nothing is more powerful than the very source of life itself. Your life source strives for expression through you. This is analogous to the great power of the unconditional love that the father had for both the prodigal son and the good son. The natural tendency of this power is to be fully expressed, and so the longing of the father in the parable is the longing of unconditional love for its fullest expression. Since this love is unconditional, it demands nothing in return.

At the same time, your primal self has the longing to be reunited with its source, as the prodigal longed to return home. "Primal" as I use the word refers not to the needy, selfish, pained, angry, sexual, or infantile characteristics which are described in some psychological systems as "primal," but rather "Primal" as the Kabbalists use the word in describing the "primal will to good." I refer to the deepest longings of human nature to reunite with its life-source. Sometimes this longing is called the "soul urge." It exists at a level deeper than your psychological makeup, deeper than your self-conscious thoughts, deeper than your intuitive perceptions, and deeper even than the structures that are predominantly in play in your life. St. Augustine referred to this longing when he observed, "Our hearts are restless until they rest in thee."

The relationship of attraction between these two forces–the source and the primal self–is itself structural in nature and generates a path of least resistance which leads these two forces to reunite.

Since both these forces operate outside the realm of time, that is, they are not time-dependent, their integration can happen at any moment, even at moments which, logically, would seem incongruous.

In the structure of cause and effect, which gives rise to events sequentially related to other events, it seems that the only possible step each new action can lead to is the next action in the cause-and-effect sequence. It therefore seems impossible for a change to occur which is unrelated to what already exists in the cause-and-effect chain.

And yet, as if miraculously and independently of normal causality, you can transcend your circumstances, your history, and the dominant structures which have been at play in your life, as well as every other aspect of your past and present. You can come home to yourself.

TRANSCENDENCE IN CIVILIZATION

Transcendence is not merely a personal principle; it can occur in civilization as a whole.

When we consider the causal forces at work in history, we might conclude that at present our civilization has a probable future of destruction, decay, and disintegration. However, in each individual on this planet there is the deepest longing to reunite with what is highest in them. Thus, transcendence for the planet as a whole becomes more and more possible as the individuals who make up civilization shift from a reactive-responsive orientation to the orientation of the creative, in which transcendence becomes the norm.

During its history, our planet has been characterized mostly by reactive-responsive people acting within the framework of structural conflict and being led through the path of least resistance from circumstance to circumstance, mostly being driven by those circumstances and hardly ever having a real vision of what they truly wanted to create.

But at this moment in our history a new door is opening, into an era motivated by vision, energized by aspiration, rooted in current reality, being forged by each creative act and leading to a transcendence of the civilization as a whole.

When historian Theodore White was asked what, in his view, was the force with the most power to shape history, he said, "The idea." He then pointed out how at different times in history different ideas have empowered great shifts in human civilization.

The idea that is currently in the air, the insight that is ripe, the principle that is the most powerful catalyst of our age is that each individual can be the predominant creative force in his or her own life.

Once you have discovered this principle for yourself, there is no turning back. Your life will be changed forever.